Sketches of Early Texas
and Louisiana

Photograph of Frédéric Gaillardet in middle life.

FRÉDÉRIC GAILLARDET

Sketches of Early
Texas and Louisiana

Translated with an Introduction and Notes by
JAMES L. SHEPHERD, III

UNIVERSITY OF TEXAS PRESS, AUSTIN & LONDON

FOR MARGUERITE CAMBIAS,

*a child of Texas and Louisiana,
from her Uncle Jimmie*

INTRODUCTION

Of the considerable number of French visitors to the Republic of Texas toward 1839, Théodore-Frédéric Gaillardet was the only professional writer of note. His remarks are therefore the most interestingly written, the best organized, the most cohesive. Their comparative neglect since their original publication is somewhat baffling when one considers the remarkable interest in Texas history and the multiplicity of publications of Texana during the past several decades. The fact that the author occupies a respected, if not a foremost, place in the history of French literature of the nineteenth century ought, one might expect, to have attracted to him the attention of Texas historians; yet one searches their works in vain for any serious treatment of his travels in Louisiana and Texas and of the writings that those travels inspired.

We propose, therefore, to take a belated look at this man and then to proceed to a consideration of the work by him which fills the pages of this book. We shall present a summary of Gaillardet's life from birth to death, a more detailed discussion of his years in North America, and finally a description of the various chapters of the book.

i

Gaillardet was a son of Burgundy, born April 7, 1808, in Tonnerre.[1] Completing his law degree in Paris, he returned in his twenties to Ton-

---

[1] According to the registry of births of the city of Tonnerre, France, Théodore-Frédéric Gaillardet was born April 7, 1808, in that city, the son of Jean-Baptiste Gaillardet and his wife Geneviève-Henry. A copy of the entry in the birth registry was graciously communicated by the mayor's office of

nerre to establish his practice. Along came the resurgence of the French theater with the first successes of Victor Hugo and Alexandre Dumas *père* to sweep Gaillardet into the current of the literary movement and forever away from the backwater of the provincial lawyer's life. Although he failed to establish himself in the first rank of Romantic dramatists, he was successful enough to have three plays from his pen produced in Parisian playhouses in the years 1832 and 1833. Dumas considerably rewrote the first of these (*La Tour de Nesle*) prior to its performance; this doubtless counted as a factor, along with Gaillardet's own talent, in making the play an enormous success. It was frequently revived throughout the nineteenth century, was twice translated into English, and is the work for which the author is chiefly remembered today. Dumas attempted to take all the credit for himself and to have Gaillardet's name stricken from the billboards; Gaillardet retaliated with a duel and more conclusive legal action.

In 1836 he published a novel in the form of memoirs of an enigmatic character in French history, the Chevalier d'Éon, an eighteenth-century foreign agent whose success as a transvestite placed him in numerous peculiar situations, including a position as favorite lady in waiting to Empress Elizabeth of Russia. This volume was well received and was a natural source of popular dramas and vaudevilles, four of which were performed simultaneously in four theaters of Paris soon after the book came out.[2]

Tonnerre; this official information was necessary in order to correct the many inaccurate statements as to the place and date of birth of the author. In none of the biographical notices we have consulted is the exact information correctly given: most state that Auxerre was the place; often the year given is 1807; when year and place are correct, the day is wrong, or no day or month is supplied.

[2] *Courrier des États-Unis,* XII (January 14, 1840), 533. Gaillardet implied in his 1836 volume that the memoirs were authentic, not fictional. When he later wished to expose a plagiary (Louis Jourdan's *Un Hermaphrodite*), he was forced to declare that a great deal of the work stemmed from his imagination. Cf. Albert Larcher, "A Propos du célèbre et énigmatique Chevalier d'Éon," p. 28.

DÉPARTEMENT
DE L'YONNE
—
ARRONDISSEMENT
D'AVALLON
—
TÉLÉPHONE 107
ET 213
—
N° 35

VILLE DE TONNERRE

EXTRAIT DU REGISTRE DES NAISSANCES
pour l'Année 1808.

L'an mil huit cent huit le huit Avril heure de dix du matin en l'Hôtel de Ville de Tonnerre chef lieu du quatrième Arrondissement de l'Yonne et pardevant nous premier adjoint Officier civil de ladite ville : Est comparu Jean Baptiste GAILLARDET marchand orphèvre âgé de vingt trois ans demeurant en cette ville, lequel nous a déclaré que le jour d'hier heure de neuf du jourest né audit Tonnerre de lui GAILLARDET et de Geneviève HENRY son épouse âgée de vingt six ans, un enfant du sexe masculin qu'il nous a présenté et auquel il a déclaré donner les prénoms de THEODORE FREDERIC, la dite déclaration de présentation faite en présence du sieur François Julien MORICE professeur de musique âgé de vingt huit ans, et Pierre Robert CHAFFAUT horloger âgé de vingt deux ans tous deux demeurant à Tonnerre qui ont signé avec nous et le déclarant après lecture faite.

— Suivent les signatures.

Délivré à Tonnerre le vingt quatre Septembre mil neuf cent soixante cinq.

Pour extrait conforme.

Le MAIRE,
Pour le Maire empêché,
L'Adjoint :

Plate 1. Extract from the birth registry of the city of Tonnerre, France, giving the official record of the place and date of birth of Frédéric Gaillardet.

After his fling in the theater, Gaillardet's career was chiefly in journalism; he became an editor of a New York newspaper and a frequent
contributor to periodicals in France. After his residence of twelve years
in North America he was brought home to France by the advent of the
Second Republic in 1848. He became a candidate for a seat in the Con-
stituent Assembly and found himself opposed by his old enemy Dumas.
The latter infuriated him by claiming in a campaign speech that Gaillardet's American sojourn had been motivated by his desire to flee from
Dumas after the *Tour de Nesle* quarrel. The accusation was a vote-
getting invention of the novelist, for which he later apologized. When
Louis-Napoleon, the future Napoleon III, entered the race also, Gaillardet withdrew his candidacy. He then resumed his long career as a
journalist, which he had never abandoned from the time he set foot in
America and which he pursued until his death. He wrote of French
affairs in his New York newspaper and of American affairs in French
papers, spanning the Atlantic with a prolific flow of popular, sensible
commentaries on the news. After his marriage he established his residence in the town of Le Plessis-Bouchard, a short distance to the northwest of Paris; there he served as mayor (1860–1870, 1876–1881). In
his last years he stole time to write chapters of a book that his death
interrupted. Essentially the memoirs of his life in America, this was to
have been also a companion piece and a corrective to Alexis de Tocqueville's *De la Démocratie en Amérique* (1835–1840). What there was
of it appeared posthumously in 1883, the year after his death, under
the appropriate title of *L'Aristocratie en Amérique*.

ii

Gaillardet traveled from France to New Orleans in 1837, having
first obtained assurance from several Parisian newspaper editors that
his contributions from America would find a place in their columns.
He was also interested in a wine-importing business to be operated in
association with one of his two brothers, both of whom accompanied
him on the Atlantic crossing. The bank failures of 1837, together with

an epidemic of yellow fever in New Orleans, caused the failure of this venture. "I then conceived the plan," he states in his memoirs, "of utilizing for literary purposes my voyage, by studying at first hand the political and social organization of the United States, a subject made popular by the fine book of Tocqueville."[3] Several side trips delayed the execution of this plan: visits to Cuba, to Texas, and up the Mississippi to Indian territory. At last he settled in New York, where he had an advantage over his contemporaries, Tocqueville, Gustave de Beaumont, and others who wrote of America on the basis of brief visits: he remained in New York for more than eight years as a student and critic of our ways. The severity of his judgments, as published in his newspaper, the *Courrier des États-Unis,* often aroused the ire of the New Yorkers; he was threatened with a lynching and with the destruction of his printing press. Yet he won the protection and friendship of many influential people, including Senator Thomas Benton of Missouri, the historian and politician Charles J. Ingersoll of Philadelphia, and Caleb Cushing, the first American commissioner to China.

Life in New York in 1840 offered problems to the young foreigner unprepared for the manifestations of an exuberant, expansive, new society, where anything could happen. To cite an example, he confesses that a parade of temperance crusaders, shortly after his arrival in the city, was one of the strangest spectacles he had ever beheld. Confronted with their distinctive dress, their crude placards and banners, their division into platoons according to age groups, and their leaflets scattering to the four winds, he reacted as a true son of Burgundy might be expected to react—he found their behavior and their cause equally ludicrous:

By a strange paradox, they could best be compared to a party of carousers flocking home at dawn on Ash Wednesday, these sallow-faced, hollow-eyed, bent-backed abstainers. Extremes meet, and surely one must judge the confirmed alcoholic to be no more guilty of excess than one who totally and

[3] Frédéric Gaillardet, *L'Aristocratie en Amérique,* p. 71.

systematically abstains from the consumption of so natural, so necessary a beverage as wine.[4]

His criticism extends to the bystanders as well. He is amazed that such proceedings could be viewed with sympathy instead of ridicule. In Europe, only hooting and scoffing would have greeted this parade, he asserts. Here, a climate of naïve tolerance permits extremist movements to attract memberships in the millions. A certain gullibility, or unquestioning simplicity, on the part of the masses, while beneficial to the working of democracy, spawns quackery as well.

Outspokenness of this caliber, from the mouth of an ousider, was bound to earn as many enmities as friendships. When Gaillardet left America, he had nonetheless established the *Courrier des États-Unis* as the leading French-language newspaper of the hemisphere, a position it continued to hold for many years thereafter. His reputation in the United States is attested by the warm letters of adieu and recommendation to our diplomatic representatives abroad, which he received in 1848 from leading citizens, including the future President James A. Buchanan. Charles J. Ingersoll especially heaped tribute upon him, both as a person and as an editor: "No American newspaper that I know of has been directed with more eminent a talent and success than his *Courrier des États-Unis.*"[5]

Gaillardet's visit to Texas in the spring of 1839 coincided with that of Admiral Charles Baudin, following the defeat of the Mexicans by the French at San Juan de Ulloa, and with that of Alphonse Dubois de Saligny, the diplomat who later became the head of the French Legation at Austin. The latter accompanied Gaillardet in his calls upon Generals Houston and Lamar and the members of Lamar's cabinet. In the company of Saligny also, Gaillardet traveled to the principal settlements of Texas; they formed a friendship that remained cordial forever afterwards. During these considerable travels (April–July, 1839), Gaillardet received a favorable impression of Texas, which was communicated to Europe in his newspaper stories. Later, he addressed to

[4] Gaillardet, *L'Aristocratie,* p. 235.
[5] Gaillardet, *L'Aristocratie,* p. 292. The letters of Buchanan and Ingersoll are given in French in their entirety, pp. 291–292.

Lamar the following letter, which we reproduce with the original spelling:

New-York, 25 November 1839

Sir,

I do not know whether you recollect a traveller who visited Texas in the month of last May, in company with Mr de Saligny, and who had the honor of being introduced to you by that gentleman. For my part, I have not forgotten that I promised to send to you the little work that I wrote for the Paris *Journal des Débats*, on the subject of Texas. I now fulfill my engagement.

My friend, Mr de Saligny, told me that my work had been of some use to the cause of Texas in France, which is a great happiness to me. In order to add, if possible, to the good effect produced by litterary essays, I have caused them to be republished in the New-York *Courrier des Etats-Unis*. This is an opportunity for me to inform you that I have recently bought this last paper. During twenty years, it has been the organe of the French population of both americas; but I want it to become as much american as it is French. For that purpose, I intend publishing very soon an other *Courrier des Etats-Unis* in English, edited by the best writers in New-York.

Both my public prints will be what I am myself—Texian in the heart, and I will feel happy every time that I will find an opportunity to prove my devotion to your country and yourself.

I am, Sir, with the highest consideration

Your most humble servant

F. GAILLARDET

Excuse, Sir, my bad English, if you please.[6]

All available evidence points to the conclusion that, by discussing and publishing his enthusiastic reactions to Texas, our "Texian in the heart" shared in bringing about French recognition of Texas's independence from Mexico. France's initiative in according this recognition well in advance of the other European powers is a fact too often forgotten and one which contributed substantially to the course of future history in the unstable young state.[7]

[6] Mirabeau B. Lamar, *The Papers of Mirabeau Buonaparte Lamar,* V, 327.
[7] George O'Brien John, we notice, sandwiches French recognition between the British and Belgian: *Texas History: An Outline,* p. 112; cf. p. 132.

iii

The neglect of articles on the history of Texas and Louisiana by so prominent an author as Gaillardet can be explained mainly by their scattered publication in newspapers on both sides of the Atlantic. We hope to correct this neglect by having assembled from several sources a colorful history that evidences a Romanticist's taste for the sensational and bizarre, and at the same time a historian's sharp insight and just appraisal of facts.

The present volume consists first of a few dispatches from Texas to Paris published in June, 1839. Five longer articles follow, those which Gaillardet enclosed with his letter to Lamar, all but one of which were reprinted, as he had planned, in the *Courrier des États-Unis*. The articles on La Salle's explorations and on the founding of New Orleans were printed in the *Courrier* as a sequel to the previous series, as was the group of vignettes of prominent Louisiana lawyers. A chapter on Champ d'Asile was drawn from a Paris paper of 1841, *Le Constitutionnel*. To complete the collection, we add a chapter on the later life of Pierre Soulé, the controversial lawyer, politician, and diplomat whom Gaillardet knew well and whose biography would remain incomplete without reference to these pages. Soulé, having previously met President Lamar, gave to both Saligny and Gaillardet letters of introduction to the President, as the two travelers set out from New Orleans for Texas in February and April, 1839, respectively. Soulé describes Gaillardet as:

. . . an intimate friend . . . a high character amongst the first writers of the modern litterature of France . . . . He will in all probability be much consulted about the report which he [Saligny] will have to send to his government on the object of his journey to Texas. Believing as I do that he will eventually have a great influence on the mind of Mr de Saligny, and considering that your growing Republic might derive great advantage from their good disposition in its favour, I have made it a duty to put Mr. Gaillardet in immediate contact with you . . .[8]

[8] Lamar, *Papers,* V, 252, 270.

Gaillardet, for his part, remained a staunch supporter of Soulé, notably during the latter's trying period as United States minister to the Court of Madrid. Of the press coverage of the various incidents in that unsuccessful mission, Soulé's biographer, A. A. Ettinger, notes that the articles by Gaillardet expressed the most uniformly sympathetic view of Soulé's actions and that his newspaper was the first to report the plan for the Ostend Conference. Ettinger ranks Gaillardet with James Gordon Bennett and Horace Greeley among the glories of New York journalism and recommends *L'Aristocratie en Amérique* as containing one of the most valuable accounts of Soulé's early life and his encounters in Madrid with the Marquis de Turgot.[9]

Throughout his book, Ettinger cites various newspaper articles by Gaillardet among his references. We have chosen instead to include here the first description that Gaillardet made of Soulé (in the chapter on the members of the New Orleans bar), with which Ettinger was apparently unfamiliar. For Soulé's subsequent activities and death, we have chosen the appropriate sections of *L'Aristocratie en Amérique* as representing Gaillardet's seasoned judgment and summation of Soulé's life and achievements. To have included *all* that he ever wrote on this one man would have been beyond the scope of this short book. The sampling that we do provide may invite a revaluation of a most arresting personality whom history has seemingly maligned. At least we have no reason to doubt Gaillardet's sincerity: in 1882, Soulé had been dead for more than ten years; his old friend could have had no other motive in defending him than to pay a final tribute to one whose abilities and character were, he believed, above reproach. Without entering into details, Gaillardet suggests that Buchanan was to blame for whatever overstepping of authority or political immorality the Ostend Manifesto represented. Soulé's chief purpose, Gaillardet states, was to assert the right of American diplomacy to lend support to revolutionary republi-

[9] Amos Aschbach Ettinger, *The Mission to Spain of Pierre Soulé, 1853–1855: A Study in the Cuban Diplomacy of the United States*, pp. 354, 511, 516. The writer erroneously states (p. 107) that Gaillardet founded the *Courrier des États-Unis* in 1828; actually, he bought it in 1839 from the heirs of the bookseller Beer, who had recently died (*L'Aristocratie*, p. 120).

cans in Europe; it was not, as it is generally assumed, to threaten Spain with an American seizure of Cuba. To what extent was Soulé the author of the latter idea as expressed in the Manifesto? Could he not have been rather the scapegoat on whom the blame was thrown as soon as it became clear that the Manifesto would receive only censure? The whole matter should be re-examined in the light of Gaillardet's testimony, for there emerge from these pages three possible, alternative conclusions: (1) Soulé mesmerized Gaillardet into a completely erroneous conception of his intentions; (2) Gaillardet rightly interpreted Soulé's motivation, and therefore the harsh judgment of history is wrong; (3) Gaillardet was secretly employed by Soulé to try to whitewash the latter's crass proposal to rob Spain of Cuba. The last hypothesis appears most improbable since, long after Soulé's death, Gaillardet was still defending him.

The four other lawyers of Lousiana whose portraits Gaillardet draws in the chaper on the members of the bar were all, like Soulé, known to him personally. The description of their various personalities and abilities, together with the anecdotes about them, constitutes a valuable source for any future biographical studies of them.

The account of Champ d'Asile, based not only upon written sources but also upon a visit that Gaillardet made to the site of this ephemeral colony, is one of the most reliable of a large number of treatments of the subject by his French contemporaries. American historians of Texas ignored the incident, which continued to fascinate the French for fifty years after the dispersal of the colony.[10]

None of our chapters has ever, to our knowledge, appeared in English translation. We present them in the order of their original publication in French, except that the first six chapters on Texas have been grouped together, as forming a connected whole, before the chapters on Louisiana. By this order, the contemporary alternates with the past; jumping back and forth from one period to another is rather a novelist's

[10] For a review of the abundant French literature and art inspired by Champ d'Asile, see René Rémond, *Les États-Unis devant l'opinion française, 1815–1852*, I, 44–56.

technique than that of the historian, but is no disservice to Gaillardet: as a journalist writing for the general reader, he often chose historical subjects and a fictional technique. The French word *vulgarisateur* describes him perfectly—a writer who can entertain a large public while disseminating reliable information. This talent is closely akin to that of Dumas, for whom Gaillardet repeatedly professed deepest admiration despite their unending clashes. Our book is not, therefore, merely for the Texas history collector or the specialist of Louisiana lore: it is intended to be of general interest.

The following liberties were taken in the translation: obvious misspellings and other misprints were corrected without notation of the original error; wherever feasible, direct quotations from English were rendered by their original English words, rather than by a retranslation from the French. For the latter purpose, the translator was obliged to seek out the English sources, for which Gaillardet gives few clues. One result of this bit of research was that Chester Newell's history of the Texas revolution emerged as the principal source on that subject. Our footnotes record evidence of the gleanings from Newell and other sources, along with references, factual precisions, and commentaries.

Gaillardet's knowledge of the English language appears to have been adequate to his purpose; we have found only a few misreadings of Newell's statements (see note 2, Chapter Four, and note 3, Chapter Six). Elsewhere, our author speaks feelingly of the difficulties of English. We conclude that he was well grounded in the written language (his letter to Lamar cited above attests to the fact); yet he found the vernacular of Louisiana and the West too full of local color to be easily assimilated. Later in life he was to deliver public addresses in English, speaking in America on behalf of Horace Greeley in the presidential campaign of 1872.

The chief historical value of this book lies in its record of Gaillardet's personal observations in Texas and Louisiana, and with Soulé in France. He excels in the anecdotal. His retelling of such familiar stories as the exploration and colonization of Louisiana, the war for Texas independence, and the taming of the mustangs has its own merits to recommend it. He culls the essential, discards inconsequential details (unless they are very entertaining), and never loses the forest for the trees. He brings vividness to his subject, if not the last shred of evidence from which his conclusions might have been drawn. Therefore, if we have rendered it faithfully, the entire set will be appreciated for its verve. The same emotional appeal is exerted in the pages that contain no new facts or interpretations as in those which reflect personal experiences. The purple passages and frequent indulgence in metaphor, not always of the most felicitous choice, will appear quaint to the present-day reader, although not, we trust, utterly rebarbative. We have made no attempt to suppress them or to tone them down in the translation, in the hope that allowances will be made both for Gaillardet's natural exuberance and for the influence of the literary tendencies of his day. Any attenuation of such color, on the part of the translator, would have been a rank betrayal.

JAMES L. SHEPHERD, III

Baylor University

CONTENTS

ILLUSTRATIONS

Sketches of Early Texas
and Louisiana

.

Urging French Recognition of Texas

JOURNAL DES DÉBATS, PARIS, JUNE 21, 1839—Editor's note:[1]
We receive from our correspondent in New Orleans, who has just returned from a visit to Texas, a report that will be read with considerable interest. The name of France, which has always been great in America, has shone with renewed luster since the capture of San Juan de Ulloa. It has already been reported with what enthusiasm the news concerning this striking feat of arms was received throughout the United States; what a welcome is daily extended to our sailors; and how the presence of a son of the King of the French [the Prince de Joinville] has been celebrated. As Texas prepares to welcome Admiral Baudin, it partakes of our joy of victory and expresses the most heartfelt satisfaction; however, its desire to win French friendship did not

[1] The author of this introductory note is Louis-François Bertin *l'Aîné* (1766–1841), the founder and editor of the *Journal des Débats.* See M. Prévost, "Bertin l'Aîné" in *Dictionnaire de biographie française.* In announcing on June 21, 1839, that Gaillardet had returned from Texas to New Orleans, Bertin is apparently premature. Gaillardet dated one article (Chapter Five of the present volume) from San Felipe de Austin, June 30, 1839. It is doubtful that he should have returned to New Orleans prior to that date.

wait for the French declaration of war on Mexico. As early as its second year of independent status, Texas sent a representative to Paris to solicit French recognition and to seal by a commercial treaty the relationship it desired to establish between France and itself. Doubtless the wisest of considerations prevented at the time any furtherance of the negotiations initiated by General Henderson, the Texian envoy; we neither recognized the new Republic nor concluded a treaty with it. Today, the circumstances which might have justified our government's refusal have been removed; we no longer have the same wariness to maintain; it would be incomprehensible for France to delay any longer in fulfilling the wishes of Texas. To do so would be something like a repetition of the mistakes committed by the Restoration government with regard to the new republics of Latin America. In vain the latter proposed to France, in exchange for the recognition of their independence, offers of treaties which later became impossible. We should be committing the same mistake without the same justification or without the same faulty reasoning. Not only is the independence of Texas established beyond controversy or reversal, but its population and prosperity are increasing with astounding speed. In the midst of all the problems of a new government, in cities just created, with all the disorder associated with its mode of formation, Texas has been organized without civil war. The same peace attended the formation of the Union of North America sixty years ago, unlike that of the former Spanish colonies. Those institutions which General Houston, the first President, failed to establish will be provided by the new President, General Lamar, a statesman who would be a credit to any country in the world. Soon this magnificent territory that the Spanish neglected and the Mexicans lost; these ports along the northern shore of the Gulf of Mexico, which are superior to Tampico and Veracruz; these great rivers which cross and fructify a virgin soil—all will be invigorated with commerce and agriculture in the hands of an energetic race who clearly know how to develop a frontier region. Such is the country for which we urge French recognition at the earliest moment. That moment could not be more opportune. If, as our correspondent states, our government has dispatched an observer there to study the resources and economic potential of the new state, we trust that this official's view will bear out our own. The report of our New Orleans correspondent follows.

HOUSTON, TEXAS, APRIL 21, 1839—After exploring part of Texas, I intended to communicate a few details concerning this admirable and interesting land. As I reach the temporary capital, Houston, I receive news which must take precedence over all else.

The first item, that which stirs and excites the city and government most, is the announcement of the probable visit of Admiral Baudin. The news originates in a letter to President Lamar from the Admiral himself, delivered by the *abbé* Anduze, the honored and learned chaplain who has graciously turned diplomatic courier for the occasion and foreign service agent if need be. To grasp the full significance of this proposed visit, it is necessary to summarize a few facts of contemporary history.

Ever since it established its *de facto* independence over a certain area, the government of Texas has sought two goals: to consolidate the independence and to enlarge the area. The first of these requires diplomatic recognition by some major European power (to date, the United States is the only country to recognize Texas). Recognition by France would be especially valuable, for it would cause Texas currency, suffering at present a devaluation of from sixty to sixty-five per cent in American markets, to quickly regain something like its par value. The only reason for its depreciation is the politically precarious condition of the country. If Texas were admitted to the rank of a nation by a leading world power, it would be able immediately to negotiate a large loan, the final signature for which depends solely on this condition. The lender or negotiator, Mr. Biddle, has stated this unequivocally.[2] That is why the Texas government has sent to Paris its

---

[2] Nicholas Biddle (1786–1844), the Pennsylvania banker, was constantly being solicited during this period for a loan to Texas. "There is combined in *him* more power and inclination to serve Texas than any other man in the United States" (H. T. Burnley and Sam M. Williams to H. Smith, Secretary

envoy, General Henderson, with the mission of soliciting the ardently
desired recognition by the Tuileries government. That is why our government, wishing to ascertain the present situation and future resources
of Texas, has sent M. de Saligny, a secretary of the Washington legation, to visit and study this country as a private citizen without official
title.[3]

To reach the second of its goals, the obtaining of certain territory
necessary to the preservation of its security and the defense of its
frontiers,[4] Texas has begun, as is customary in any legal dispute, by
sending a formal petition to the opposing side, Mexico. To this effect
Colonel [Barnard E.] Bee has recently been sent to Mexico City.
Colonel Bee was one of two officials who, in 1836, accompanied Santa
Anna to Washington, to explore the means of obtaining recognition
of independence from Mexico with the help of Santa Anna, their
prisoner. It will be remembered that the life of the latter had been
spared in return for this promise of independence, but that he could
not keep his word, as he was thrown out of power immediately by his
country. Today, with Santa Anna again in the presidency, Texas is
reminding him of his promise and asking him to keep it in a way that
will wound neither his pride nor that of Texas. It does not openly

of the Treasury, October 8, 1838, in *Texas Treasury Papers: Letters Received in
the Treasury Department of the Republic of Texas, 1836–1846,* ed. Seymour V.
Connor, Virginia H. Taylor, I, 137). "The recognition of independence by
England would insure the loan immediately" (letter of H. T. Burnley, August
8, 1837, ibid., IV, 29).

[3] Jean-Pierre-Isidore-Alphonse Dubois de Saligny (1812–1888) served in the
diplomatic corps at Hanover and in Greece before coming to the United States
in 1833. His exploratory mission to Texas, 1838–1839, was followed by his
appointment as chargé d'affaires, a post he occupied for five years: 1839–1842;
1844–1845. For details of his life in Texas, see Marcel Moraud, "The Diplomatic Relations of the Republic of Texas," *The Rice Institute Pamphlet,* XLIII
(October, 1956), 29–54. Concerning James Pinckney Henderson's diplomacy in
Europe, see Mary Katherine Chase, *Négociations de la République du Texas en
Europe, 1837–1845,* pp. 15–49.

[4] "This territory is located between the Nueces River, which is the present
boundary of Texas, and the great river named Río Grande or Río Bravo del
Norte" (Gaillardet's note; footnotes by the author will be identified henceforth
by the abbreviation GN).

solicit the recognition of its independence. Shrewdly aware that this is unimportant as a bone of contention, it rather offers to buy a strip of land. The acceptance of this offer will, it figures, imply recognition of its rights as an independent nation.

That this negotiation will be successful I seriously doubt. What I do believe and what Texians are saying is that they will gain control of the territory in question by force if need be.

With a view of this eventuality, they have addressed, or caused to be addressed, to the French government a second petition after the one which requests recognition as a sovereign state. This is an offer and proposal to call to arms a body of fifteen thousand men, to launch an offensive attack on Mexico in the common interest of France and Texas. We, in return for this military aid, would furnish arms and munitions, repayment for which would be guaranteed by a lien on the public lands. The peace which we have just signed with the Mexican government renders this action unnecessary for us at present.

Meanwhile, Admiral Baudin determined to find out what the Texians might do if called upon in the future. He therefore resolved to stop to visit this country, which offers much of interest from various standpoints. However, in announcing to General Lamar not his arrival but the possibility that he might make a call during his eastward journey, Baudin was careful to insist repeatedly upon the fact that he would come without any governmental orders, without any official character. "I shall merely observe and report," he stated.

Regardless of the truth of these reservations, the people and government interpreted them as nothing more than the usual cautious language of diplomacy. A paroxysm of joy seized them, and at once orders were issued for a reception worthy of the victor of Ulloa and, what was more important to them, the representative of France. As tomorrow is the anniversary of the Battle of San Jacinto, the establishment of Texas independence, it is hoped that the Admiral can arrive in time for the ball, and in this expectation an invitation has just been printed for him in letters of gold on watered satin. The cannon of the city are all loaded and ready for firing. The good people of Texas would indeed be disappointed if the Admiral did not make it; to tell the truth, I do not much expect that he will.

Moreover, upon his arrival, the Admiral will find that his way has been paved with perfect tact and felicity by the envoy of our government, Monsieur de Saligny. The latter doubtless came with less explicit instructions than the Admiral will have. He has confined himself to making personal contacts with the numerous citizens to whom he has access. The reserve which he displayed in his encounters with the politicians of Texas had the fortunate effect of stimulating their desires; spontaneous offers of special advantages came in direct proportion to the coolness of the French agent. The recent announcement has thus been doubly intoxicating to them by virtue of its unexpectedness. It will be up to the Admiral, if he does visit them, to temper this premature jubilation. With the eminent tact and noble instincts which characterize him, he will know how to reduce to reality these immoderate expectations, or else to use them for the commercial and political advantage of France.

Concerning Admiral Baudin, I could relate many creditable facts, but I think that you are already familiar with most of them. Before leaving Veracruz, the Admiral placed in the care of the local priest a sum of money to be divided among the needy Mexican families who suffered most from the blockade and the evacuation of the city. Father Anduze describes with warmth the thanksgiving which the Veracruzanos expressed to the Admiral. He confirms to me the fact, already reported in the papers, that the inhabitants were resolved to float the French flag over Veracruz and to place themselves under the Admiral's protection if the peace treaty were not ratified by the Mexican Congress. Already a junta had been formed for this purpose, when news of the ratification reached them.

GALVESTON, APRIL 23, 1839—Last night I left Houston on a steamboat to visit San Jacinto Battleground, located between Houston and Galveston and therefore on the route which Admiral Baudin is expected to follow. It was midnight when the steamboat reached the plain known to the Texians as the Battleground. It is immediately below the point where the small stream called Buffalo Bayou joins the larger San Jacinto River. No sooner had we arrived at this scene of recent glory and importance for Texians than the passengers, who filled the steamer to capacity, broke forth into frenzied shouting, mingled with artillery fire and military band music. It was a curious spectacle to witness, this really terrifying explosion of patriotic enthusiasm! The weather was superb. The inhabitants of the plain, aroused by the unexpected cannonade from the river, hastened to light up their windows and to run half-naked to the little row of cannon on the bank, which they proceeded to shoot off. Soon we went ashore, and the patriotic throng, armed with resin torches, formed a fiery frame around the field. There the famous patriotic song "Yankee Doodle" was sung, and the ceremony concluded with three cheers, shouted in not inharmonious chorus by the exultant crowd, who, with this triple adieu, honored the memory of their heroes who had died for their country.

This morning I went ashore in Galveston, the chief port of Texas. Admiral Baudin had not yet appeared. I am leaving the expectant city and am resuming my travels.[5]

Yet, I shall not bring this article to a close without saying a word

[5] Gaillardet's travels in Texas between April 23 and May 23 cannot be accurately traced from the internal evidence of this book. It is known that he had met Saligny in New Orleans and that, upon arrival in Houston, the two waited in vain for Baudin's promised appearance; when they had given up all hope of his coming they agreed to explore a part of Texas together. Specifically, they visited the timber resources (Chapter Six) and Champ d'Asile (Chapter Ten). Gaillardet states: "Saligny very graciously offered me his services, and together we visited the most interesting localities, among others the famous Champ d'Asile" (*L'Aristocratie en Amérique*, p. 76). There is no evidence of Saligny's having encountered Baudin in Texas, as suggested by Moraud ("Diplomatic Relations," p. 35), who places Baudin's visit one year earlier (May, 1838, instead of 1839); elsewhere, Moraud places Gaillardet's visit to Champ d'Asile as early as 1837 ("Le Champ d'Asile au Texas," *The Rice Institute Pamphlet*, XXXIX [April, 1952], 44). Doubtless these inaccuracies are typographical errors.

about the admirable conduct of our sailors during the recent fire in
Veracruz and about the favorable impression they made on the Mexicans, creating sympathy toward the French in general. The other
foreigners, who witnessed the disaster with indifference, could not
understand or emulate such heroism. A Texian who has recently returned from Veracruz has described to me this incident and its effect
on the people of Veracruz in terms of such flattery and admiration for
Admiral Baudin and for his brave seamen that I cannot resist the
pleasure of passing the news on in this report to you.[6]

GALVESTON, TEXAS, MAY 23, 1839—Texas has finally entertained Admiral Baudin after long and eager expectation. He was received with indescribable joy and enthusiasm. I was at that time far
from the capital, deep in the Texas woods.[7] When I returned to Houston, the Admiral had already departed; but the thrill of his visit still
lingered among the Texians, and the city was abuzz with talk of the
great event. Texians attach great importance indeed to this visit from
the Admiral. One of their newspapers said this morning: "We are as
good as recognized by France. General Lamar was treated by Admiral
Baudin as the President of the Republic of Texas, and the French
squadron returned our salute shot for shot."

On leaving Houston, the Admiral was obliged to visit the San
Jacinto Battleground, escorted by two Texas officers. From there he
went to Galveston, where his entertainment was no less lavish than at
Houston and Velasco. Two dinners were given in his honor, one by an

---

[6] This incident occurred April 8, 1839, and is recorded in greater detail by
Admiral Baudin's aid-de-camp Eugène Maissin, in *The French in Mexico and
Texas (1838–1839)*, pp. 124–126. The reader is referred to that volume for a
complete account of Baudin's expedition to Mexico and of his subsequent calls
in Texas, Florida, and Cuba.

[7] While Gaillardet and Saligny were exploring the hinterland, Maissin,
Baudin, and their entourage entered Texas at Velasco, reached Houston on
May 8 and Galveston, May 13. The delay in reaching Texas was owing to the
protracted peace negotiations with the Mexican government (Maissin, *French
in Mexico*, pp. 139–141).

elderly Texas general and the other by the American consul.[8] The City Council, by a unanimous decision, bestowed upon the Admiral the title of honorary citizen of Galveston. We reproduce the letter sent to the Admiral on this subject, signed by the mayor and all the aldermen:

GALVESTON CITY
TO HIS EXCELLENCY,

The Admiral Baudin . . .: We, the Mayor and Aldermen of the City of Galveston, in Council assembled, in consideration of your gallant deportment at the siege and capture of St. John de Ulloa, and your subsequent humane treatment of your prisoners, are induced to offer you the freedom of our City, and with it the good feelings of our fellow citizens and wishes for your future prosperity and happiness.
May [13], 1839

The Admiral replied with the following letter, which caused a sensation in Texas and will cause an equal one when published elsewhere, so explicit and stripped of all diplomatic reserve are its terms:

To the Honorable
The Mayor and Aldermen of the City of Galveston
Gentlemen,

With the deepest sense of gratitude I do accept the honour you have been pleased to confer upon me, in presenting me the freedom of this city of Galveston. I am glad that what I have done in Mexico has proved beneficial to so just and so sacred a cause as that of the independence of the Texian nation: I hope it will prove too beneficial to the several nations who, either as friends or as foes, have to deal with Mexico. Nothing could be more gratifying to my feelings than to be considered as one of you, Gentlemen, whose industry and energy I do admire so much. Be assured that I would vastly prefer being the humblest member of a well regulated and thriving

[8] These were Moseley Baker and Stewart Newell, respectively (Maissin, *French in Mexico,* p. 248). Baker was in his late thirties; Gaillardet's notion of age is occasionally faulty (see below, Chapter Five, note 5; Chapter Seven, note 5; Chapter Ten, note 3).

community, like yours, to moving in the sphere of wealth and power in a corrupt and decaying society.

• With the highest regard and respect I have the honour to be,

> Gentlemen,
> Your affectionate and devoted servant,
> CHARLES BAUDIN

Galveston, May 13, 1839

The following day, according to the Galveston newspaper report:

The Texian steam frigate Zavala carried the Admiral out to sea, to his ship, the Neriad, accompanied by a large number of ladies and gentlemen. As the Zavala approached, salutes were exchanged by the respective vessels, and the five hundred fifty men of the Neriad spread themselves among the rigging, teeming in every direction like a swarm of bees and gave three hearty cheers, which were responded to from the Zavala, which then came to anchor, and those on board were transported to the Neriad in small boats. The fine model and elegant condition of the Neriad, and the excellent discipline of her men, was the subject of universal remark. A splendid banquet was immediately set, and the Admiral gave the most unremitted personal attention to his guests; . . . they bid him a reluctant farewell, to return to the city. Shortly after the sails of his ship were spread, and we saw her depart for Havana, accompanied by the armed brig Curossier [*Cuirassier*] and steamship Phaeton.[9]

The outcome of the conferences which the Admiral held with President Mirabeau B. Lamar of Texas has not been made public. The Admiral failed to meet in Houston either the envoy from our Washington legation, Secretary Saligny, or his own envoy, the *abbé* Anduze. Both had departed after more than two weeks of waiting in vain for his arrival.

---

[9] *Galveston Civilian,* reprinted in Maissin, *French in Mexico,* pp. 247–249.

CHAPTER TWO

Invasions of the Anglo-American
Race into Texas[1]

VELASCO, MAY 25, 1839—Texas interests us at present in more ways than one. As a stimulus to the imagination and the curiosity of the visitor, the country offers a spectacle which will always fascinate wherever independence and civilization are brand new. An invading people, scarcely settled in their conquest, are consumed by the arduous travail of their national birth and are struggling between a past which is henceforth overcome and a future which is yet to be won. Indeed,

---

[1] Under this title the present chapter first appeared in the *Journal des Débats* on October 1, 1839. Dated only two days after the preceding dispatch, its publication was held up until after the recognition of Texas by France on September 25. This is the first of four chapters reproduced in the *Courrier des États-Unis*, XII, Nos. 71–74 (November, 1839). Bertin *l'Aîné* introduced the October series with the following paragraph, which we translate from the *Journal des Débats* of October 1, 1839: "The recent act by which the French government has definitively ratified the recognition of Texas casts a new degree of interest upon any information that can be obtained concerning the origin and history of this newborn nation. One of our correspondents has sent us a series of articles written in Texas in anticipation of the event which has just transpired to cement the relations between the two countries. We publish today the first of this series."

Texians have to the rear their former masters, the Mexicans, and to the fore their present enemies, the Indians. They must forge their way and carve their realm through a land that must be wrested from two equally stubborn adversaries. The history of this dual conflict contains some bloody episodes in its brief annals; it includes terror-filled, emotion-packed tragedies of which the European world has thus far had little inkling. The latter was too far removed from the events, both in space and in preoccupations, to have focussed attention on dramas that were enacted in an unknown wilderness on the banks of the Brazos or the San Jacinto. Thus the new epic of Texas, the chronicles so recently written and the legends so vibrantly alive with yesterday's happenings, exerts upon the tourist who wanders here the magic of a new lore and of an unmatched poetry. The names of the Milams, Travises, Fannins, and Bowies—those popular heroes of the Texian Iliad—recall to mind repeatedly and amazingly the most stalwart heroes of Homer; the fortnight of the siege of the Alamo can scarcely be paralleled by any days of the ten-year siege of Troy.

From the commercial and political points of view, Texas is no less interesting an object of study. It has unquestionably obtained its freedom and therefore its place in the rank of independent states. The time has come for other countries on either side of the Atlantic to investigate the wisdom of recognizing and sanctioning by official acts this *de facto* independence. Involved here is an opportunity of considerable importance already, and of even greater importance in the future, to that European nation which will take the lead and enlightened initiative to seize the chance being offered. The United States long ago reached its decision in the matter. It had no problem, really. The conquest was viewed by Americans as something like a national legacy. Yet even if family ties had not prompted them to a quick decision, their concern for their best interests would have led them to it. World trade is the great joiner of peoples today, the sure and durable basis for natural alliances. Americans, those avid fortune seekers, develop trade wherever they can. Little wonder that they were first to recognize Texas!

Would France be well advised to follow suit today? It is with this question that the present series of articles attempts to deal. I recognize the gravity and urgency of my task. Within recent weeks, it will be recalled, the Texian government dispatched General Henderson as minister plenipotentiary to the Court of France. The diplomatic mission of this official was to propose a commercial treaty to our leaders and to obtain, if possible, the recognition of Texas independence. The commercial treaty was brought about; as for the other matter, the French government deemed it premature or else deemed itself insufficiently informed. It ordered one of its legation secretaries to visit the country and to make a thorough first-hand investigation. This was Monsieur de Saligny, one of the most highly respected members of the Embassy in Washington. With his report, our cabinet will be able to decide and to act with a knowledge of the whole story.[2]

At the same time, I myself, an isolated pilgrim wandering over these same Texas plains, had the good fortune to confront my own modest, private observations with the expert investigations of the astute diplomat who had arrived from Washington. I should feel all the more fortunate if my personal impressions were in conformity with his, and if, after having parted company, we were destined to meet again in the similarity of the conclusions we had reached.

Texas occupies a vast and beautiful site on the Gulf of Mexico between its two neighbors, the United States and Mexico. It extends from the twenty-seventh to the thirty-eighth degree of latitude and from the ninety-fifth to the one-hundredth degree of longitude west of the Greenwich meridian. Its area is approximately four hundred square miles,[3] with a coastline of about three hundred miles. Its boundaries are, to the north, the Red River, which separates it from the state of Arkansas; to the south, the Gulf of Mexico; to the east, the Sabine River, which separates it from Louisiana; to the west, the Nueces River, which separates it from the states of Coahuila and Tamaulipas, and

---

[2] Saligny's report was dated May 21, 1839. Cf. Mary Katherine Chase, *Négociations de la République du Texas en Europe, 1837–1845,* p. 35.

[3] Cf. below, Chapter Six, note 3.

which has remained the unofficial boundary between it and Mexico.[4] Under the rule of the latter, Texas first belonged to the province of Coahuila, forming with it a single state of the Mexican confederation. In this geographical position, it was inevitable that the rich land should become the object of conquest of its enterprising neighbors to the north. It will be of value for us to go back to the first encroachments of the Anglo-American race upon Texas soil and to sketch in the causes which were at the origin of this movement.

The invasion of Texas by the Americans who today possess the land constitutes the first clash of modern times between the two races that share the Americas: the English and the Spanish. In the view of all observers, judges, and forecasters, this invasion is the first step of an irresistible and, one might say, providential outburst which is to result in the occupation of the entire North American continent by one single people. The desiccated, sapless race of the Hispano-Americans will be submerged by loamy, fertile outflow of the Anglo-American race. Sensing this mission of regenerative conquest in the future annals of his country's history, President Jefferson wrote the following significant words in 1820 to one of his nephews, who was setting out to complete his education at the University of Cambridge:

One word of advice I cannot urge too strongly upon you is that you should pay most particular attention to the study of Spanish. This tongue is spoken on our continent through a vast and rich area which the Anglo-American race is destined to occupy within a quarter of a century.[5]

[4] "Many recent books extend the area of Texas to the Río Grande. This is an error. The independence and consequently the sovereignty of Texas do not extend at present beyond the banks of the Nueces" (GN).

[5] This letter is not included in the published correspondence of Thomas Jefferson. However, it accurately expresses Jefferson's view at the time on the subject of our "manifest destiny"; cf. the following passage from a letter to James Monroe, May 14, 1820: "To us the province of Techas will be the richest State of our Union, without any exception. Its southern part will make more sugar than we can consume, and the Red River, on its north, is the most luxuriant country on earth" (*The Writings of Thomas Jefferson,* XV, 251).

Similar advice to a nephew, Peter Carr, was written by Jefferson a generation earlier (August 10, 1787): "Spanish. Bestow great attention on this, and

Less than sixteen years elapsed after this prediction before the settlement of the victorious Americans in Texas had in great part demonstrated its prophetic accuracy.

It is instructive to examine the causes of the constant expansion of one race and the progressive enfeeblement of the other, both of them having ancestors in the same hemisphere, both of them equally strong and powerful at the outset.

The English and the Spanish, today the Americans and the Mexicans, both migrated with the same object in view: the conquest of a foreign land. At the very core of this community of efforts, however, existed a basic distinction which it is important to draw. The drives which pushed the one race were not the same as those which pushed the other; they differed as to the pressure to leave home and as to the ultimate goal. The Spaniard, being satisfied or at least undisturbed at home, set out for the New World of his own free will. What made him leave? Ambition. What did he seek? Gold for himself, new possessions for his king, new converts for his church. How, moreover, did he propose to win in the New World the fortune that he expected? By trade? He scorned that. By agriculture? He despised it. He went not as a colo-

---

endeavor to acquire an accurate knowledge of it. Our future connections with Spain and Spanish America will render that language a valuable acquisition" (*The Papers of Thomas Jefferson*, XII, 14).

Jefferson's 1820 prediction of Anglo-American occupation of Texas within a quarter of a century was used as an epigraph to a work published in 1841, H. Fournel's *Coup d'œil historique et statistique sur le Texas*. Fournel concludes this volume with a further reference to the prediction, to which he adds his own dream of the erection of a statue of Moses Austin in the heart of Mexico City, to symbolize North American domination of Mexico. It is probable that Fournel borrowed the Jefferson quotation from Gaillardet.

Jefferson's spelling of the word Texas (letter of May 14, 1820, above) approximates the sound of the original Indian word better than the Spanish spelling that has now become standard: "The tribes of this [Hasinai] confederation called each other *Taychas,* meaning 'allies' or 'friends,' and the Spaniards . . . soon came to employ the word for these and other friendly natives. Probably the pronunciation of the term was closer to Tayshas or Taychas than to Texas," states W. W. Newcomb, Jr. (*The Indians of Texas: From Prehistoric to Modern Times,* p. 280).

nizer but as a soldier. He went not to cultivate the land with a slow, laborious hand, but to exploit it with an impatient arm. He sought not its harvests but its entrails. What he needed was gold, not bread; a fortune for the taking, not for the making. Later, once this fortune was seized at sword's point and by the sweat of the Negro, his human tool, the Spaniard dozed in his ease and abundance, his pride, and his prejudice.

The Anglo-American, when he gave up his native heath, did so not merely to seek his fortune but, above all, in pursuit of liberty. He lacked liberty. The religious wars in England had left him defeated: America today is populated by numerous such defeated ones. The endless lines of Protestant sects went there, far from persecution, to establish their stubbornly held beliefs on free soil. The victims of intolerance were themselves intolerant and proved to be, from the start, no less fanatical than the Spanish. Their fanaticism, however, was in words rather than deeds. The Spanish exterminated whoever refused to be converted; Anglo-Americans are content to preach to them and seize their homeland. The Spaniard left home armed with the sword of El Cid and the Madonna of his convent. The Englishman migrated with a plow and a Bible. The one came to conquer, the other to colonize. The one responds to the appeal in religion to the heart and eye, the other to that which appeals to the mind and reason. The one grasps intuitively, the other examines and judges; for the one, dogma is all, for the other, morality. Thus placed on different paths by their opposing natures, the one will attain, through the very number and variety of his religious sects, a civilization grounded in logic; the other, benumbed and blinded by the very density and unanimity of his faith, will not get beyond the superstition which breeds fanaticism and barbarity.

It results from the respective positions of the two races that the Spanish-American must tend to grow progressively weaker and to disappear, while the Anglo-American strengthens and spreads itself. Added to that, the special inborn traits of fearlessness and ambition which characterize the Anglo-American seem to be the providential sign with which heaven has marked the brow of these pioneers as they push forward the bounds of civilization. Consider what they have won and overcome, step by step across America for the past fifty years; consider what they stand yet to gain! Then with President Jefferson you too will say: "Within the next quarter of a century, this continent will be occupied by the Anglo-American race!" Europe alone, by casting its protective aegis over the weak side, and by stepping into the struggle with arms or negotiation, can halt this fatal march of destiny. If we should choose to do so, Mexico's chief threat, Texas, might conceivably become the chief instrument of its survival. Our wisest political moves under the circumstances will be discussed later at a more opportune moment. I first have to speak of Texas in the past and the present before concerning myself with its future.

The first indications that the Americans might consider Texas as a field for expansion appeared soon after the cession of Louisiana by France. The treaty of cession had not defined with any great precision the borders of the territory being ceded. It appears that Bonaparte had wished, by this very obscurity, to point the way for the Americans, whose future aspirations he could sense. One of his negotiators had indeed thought it his duty to warn him of the vagueness in the wording. He replied: "If there were no obscurity in it, good politics would demand that some be inserted." A word to the wise was sufficient: the Americans soon displayed their argumentative skill in laying claim to parts of Texas. This despite the well-recognized fact that the French colonization and property rights, from which the American rights devolved, had never extended beyond the Sabine River.

Food for the national ambition was furnished by the boundary discussions. The greed for land was whetted, and might have led to a major conflict between Spain and the United States, had not the latter's attention been diverted and absorbed by an internal security problem much more urgent of solution. I refer to the famous conspiracy of Aaron Burr, whose ranks had been strengthened by promise of the conquest of Mexico, among other grandiose schemes, so strong a temptation and so heartfelt a wish had the possession of the land to the south already become in the minds of the American people.[6]

The invasion under consideration by the Americans was then postponed and later forgotten.

The war cries which rang out in 1810 with the first move for Mexican independence reawakened old dreams that the Americans held dear. They were led to take part in the ensuing struggle, whether by a lust for adventure, by their liberal political convictions, or by the lure of profits for self and country.

In consequence, while Don José María Morelos picked up the insurrectional flag that had fallen from the hands of the monk [Miguel] Hidalgo, and held on to this flag with prodigious valor—defending it for five years with the aid of Guadalupe Victoria, [Martín] Cos, and brave [José Álvarez de] Toledo—at the same time American adventurers embraced his cause and struck at the Spanish regime through Texas.

"The origin of this expedition," says the judge and historian Brackenridge, "was far from glorious or brilliant, but that cannot lessen the interest of its history; if it was begun by men who were outlaws, it was continued by noble and intrepid souls, who were drawn from the most respectable families of the southwestern States."[7]

At the end of the year 1812, the American lieutenant [Augustus

---

[6] "Aaron Burr, with a brilliant though unstable mind, eloquent lips, and boundless ambition, had been Jefferson's opponent for the Presidency of the United States. Upon his defeat, he resolved to be the independent, personal creator of a new power equal to that which he had lost. He envisioned a split in the Union and the formation of a Republic of the West, including a defeated Mexico! This dream might have become, at least in part, a reality, except for the vigilance and energy which Jefferson marshaled against this evil genius" (GN).

[7] Henry Marie Brackenridge (1786–1871), son of the novelist Hugh Henry Brackenridge (*Modern Chivalry*), served as district judge in Louisiana until the War of 1812; he was also a judge in Florida until 1832. His *Views of Louisiana* (Pittsburgh, 1814) and his article in Robert Walsh's *American Register* (1817) contain discussions of boundary questions between Texas and Louisiana and of invasions from the United States into New Spain.

William] Magee was assigned by the national army of the United States to be the head of a military force with an official mission of dispersing a group of bandits whose headquarters were on the banks of the Sabine River and who held up the frequent commercial caravans which traveled between the city of Natchitoches and the interior provinces of New Spain.

While he was engaged in this difficult expedition Magee conceived on his own, it is said, the bold project of invading Mexico, not as an aid to one of the two sides which disputed the country, but in order to conquer it, taking advantage of its civil dissension and of the help of the very pirates he had been ordered to subdue. The latter readily fell in with his plans. With an agreement reached and a meeting place set, Magee set out for New Orleans, where he secured supplies and engaged a band of adventurers. He there met a Mexican refugee named Bernardo,[8] who had participated in the first attempt at independence with the monk Hidalgo. Magee decided to use the name of Bernardo as a cloak beneath which to conceal his own foreign nationality and his purpose of conquest—Bernardo was a necessary mask. He bought Bernardo; then he set up his tent on the bank of the Trinity and issued a proclamation in Spanish, in Bernardo's name, inviting the Mexicans to rally beneath his flag.

His first military maneuver was directed against the town of Nacogdoches, which he easily captured. There he found plentiful supplies.

News of his success soon spread through the southwest of the United States; his forces quickly grew, and in a short time they numbered five hundred men, including three hundred Americans. With no more than these, he took possession of the city of La Bahía; but soon he was besieged by an army of fifteen hundred under the command of the Spaniard [Manuel] Salcedo. The siege lasted throughout the winter of 1812–1813; scarcely a day elapsed without a skirmish, which always turned out to the advantage of the besieged. The Spanish withdrew.

---

[8] Gaillardet uses only the Christian name in referring to Bernardo Gutiérrez de Lara, as he uses only the family names of Magee, Lockett, Perry, and others.

Magee was already dead, but *not before having received a promotion from the cabinet in Washington.* His death caused dissension among the coalition of American and Spanish under his orders.

First, the command fell to the American, Lockett.[9] This skillful leader resolved not to allow the budding fortune of American arms to go unexploited. It was not enough that the Spanish had withdrawn; they must be pursued. He caught up with them six miles away from San Antonio—their garrison post—defeated them decisively, and entered the city in their stead.

Bernardo had been content to be the figurehead and during the battle had played the part of Sancho Panza, according to Judge Brackenridge. In San Antonio, however, Bernardo conceived the notion of becoming a real leader. He claimed the authority which he had held theretofore in name only. It was necessary to humor him. His first act was the massacre of seventeen Spanish officers, who had been taken prisoner. He did this contrary to the wishes of the Americans, who were outraged by the atrocity and who disclaimed any share in the moral responsibility. Lockett and several other American officers abandoned the cause which they now deemed dishonored, and they returned to their homes. The previous successes of this small band of adventurers, however, had drawn to them a large number of volunteers, who more than made up for the departure of a few officers. With the number increased by the new enlistments, the army corps was divided in two. One half, composed of seven hundred Mexicans, was placed under the command of the Spaniard [Miguel] Menchaca; the other, made up of Americans, was under Colonel [Henry] Perry. The two leaders, each at the head of his own nationals, soon won a new victory over the Spanish general, [Ignacio] Elizondo. This, however, was their last.

---

[9] Gaillardet's information regarding the successor to Magee is at variance with that of modern historians. Henry P. Walker succinctly states the facts, according to the best evidence now available: "In February, 1813, Colonel Magee died and was succeeded in command by Lieutenant Colonel Samuel Kemper" ("William McLane's Narrative of the Magee-Gutierrez Expedition, 1812–1813," *Southwestern Historical Quarterly,* LXVI [October, 1962], 239; see also p. 458).

Another leader, brave Toledo, was called by the vote of the Americans to have control of one-third of the invading army. Menchaca, jealous of this rival, betrayed him at the first opportunity. Ignoring the agreed plan of action and the orders issued to him, he set out from his position, struck forward, and fell into an ambush. Torn limb from limb by the Spanish, he caused the defeat of Toledo, too. This double disaster broke up the invading army, whose members were dispersed. Leaders and soldiers alike fled homeward.

If this disastrous battle had been deferred [states one American historian], or if the orders of Toledo had been carried out by the traitorous Menchaca, *the war which began on the Texas border would have ended in the very heart of Mexico*. At the time that the defeat became known, the San Antonio road was literally swarming with adventurers desiring to cast their vagabond lot with that of their bold compatriots. [Probably quoted from Brackenridge]

In the contest between the Mexicans and their neighbors in the United States, this was but a temporary lull.

CHAPTER THREE

Moving toward Revolution[1]

BRAZORIA, MAY 27, 1839—The first incursions of Americans into Mexican territory had as their excuse, or their impetus, the outbreak of civil war in the very heart of the country, under Hidalgo and Morelos, the first martyrs to Mexican independence. After the bloody death of Morelos and the defeat of the American adventurers, Mexico reverted to the uncontested control of the Spanish government. For six more years the weight of this authority was to be accepted without any effort to shake it (1815–1821). The Americans, during this period, except for a few bandits and pirates, respected the boundaries of their Spanish neighbors, and a degree of harmony prevailed between them.

In 1819 Spain ceded Florida to the Washington government and insisted upon a clause in the treaty whereby the United States relinquished all claims it might have asserted to the regions beyond the Sabine River. In this way, every existing ripple of dispute between the two countries was ironed out.

[1] The ideas expressed in this chapter concerning the motives of the Mexican government for encouraging colonization of Texas by immigrants from the United States are borrowed from the work by Chester Newell, *History of the Revolution in Texas*, pp. 14–15.

Texas at this time numbered only a few hundred foreigners within its territory, scattered and isolated in the vast wilderness, having come from every land and speaking every tongue. The Spanish themselves occupied only two or three small garrisons here and there in the small towns of San Antonio de Béxar, La Bahía, and Nacogdoches.

A rich and enterprising farmer of the state of Missouri, Moses Austin, got the idea of leading some Americans to Texas to found a colony. This was conquest not by war but by peace. Austin left Missouri in December, 1820, and proceeded to San Antonio de Béxar. After delays, born of the instinctive Spanish distrust and dislike of foreigners, his request was granted on January 17, 1821. The motives for which the Spanish government adopted this radically new and liberal policy of such fatal consequences are not hard to explain. By permitting foreign colonization in Texas, the Spaniards hoped to erect a living wall against the Indians, who were constantly ravaging the frontiers of Mexico without any effective resistance to their costly inroads. These inroads sometimes went south of the Río Grande; the frontier posts of Béxar and Goliad and the entire western boundary had long been heavily hit. The Americans might thus become for them and for the whole country a valuable buffer, purchased for a scrap of land that was at the time of no value whatsoever.

Texas, moreover, could only benefit agriculturally and in progress of every sort at the hands of skilled colonists. The liberalism of the Spanish with regard to the Americans was in reality a desire to exploit them. All the advantages and none of the dangers were foreseen.

Moses Austin was at first authorized to introduce no more than three hundred families, who would be subject to the following provisions: they must be composed of Catholics and for this reason be drawn largely from Louisiana; the colonists were to build churches and found schools; their children were to be reared in the Catholic faith and be taught the Spanish language.

In return, the colonists were guaranteed the dual protection of their persons and their property. An important part of what constituted their property was the slaves, whom the colonists were allowed to bring to Texas "until the year 1827 only." While permitting the importation of slaves, the law forbade slave trading and the colonists were required to set free at the age of fourteen all children born of slaves on Texas soil.

In addition, the colonists had the right to import free of duty whatever tools were necessary for the establishment of their homes. In the case of the immigration of a whole family, merchandise to a maximum value of two thousand pesetas (roughly ten thousand francs) was permitted.

Tracts of land, varying in area with the type of occupation and the needs of the immigrants, were to be sold at a cost never before as low in other colonizing enterprises.

Finally, a special law extended these privileges to the year 1840, offering them to immigrants of every nationality, provided that "no impelling necessity forced the government to cancel the rights with regard to a given nationality." The latter clause is noteworthy.

Moses Austin died before he could profit from the rights which had been granted him. As he died, he bequeathed the project he had conceived to his son Stephen Austin and enjoined him both as a patriotic and as a filial obligation to bring it to reality. Stephen Austin kept his word to his dying father: he traveled to Texas, which he regarded as a sort of patrimony; explored its vast extent without a guide and in the face of countless dangers; chose the site from which he would launch his colonizing movement; returned to the United States; enlisted some well-disposed adventurers; arrived with them in December, 1821, on the banks of the River Brazos; and began his first colony.

For six consecutive years the colony tirelessly and successfully pursued its gigantic task. No incident occurred to interrupt the peace or to alter the relationship with the central government, or rather, the central governments, of Mexico. Mexico's political situation had indeed been shaken and radically changed by many revolutions. Texas, by its indifference and its peripheral location, was placed outside the struggle; the various upheavals left it unaffected. The first and most important of these was the expulsion of Spanish rule from the Mexican states and the proclamation by [Agustín de] Iturbide of Mexican independence. Iturbide quickly seized the crown and power which had toppled under the force of his arms (1821–1822). His short-lived empire was replaced by twenty regimes, all of them weak and anarchical, before the central government could be consolidated.

This period of violence and anarchy stretched out too long before the eyes of the Americans in Texas for them not to become horrified and disgusted at such a disastrous display of ineffectuality. Their minds began to entertain thoughts of separation.

A wild, premature outbreak gave the alarm to the Mexican government, and soon Texas was overrun with troops that had trickled in, in small detachments under various pretexts. Now it was 20 men to guard a caravan, later to be joined by 40 more for a different purpose; none ever departed. They were spread about in corps of from 50 to 250 men. Nacogdoches and other garrisons had thus gradually become well manned when, in 1829, President [Vicente] Guerrero issued a proclamation freeing all slaves residing on Mexican soil. Emancipation was in direct violation of the terms under which Texas had been colonized. A mass protest was sent from Texas to the abolitionist president, who was persuaded after lengthy deliberations to exclude Texas from his decree. This arrangement was largely the work of [Ramón] Músquiz, the Mexican governor of the state of Texas and Coahuila.

A new act, no less offensive to the national pride if not to the material interests of the Texas colonists, soon reopened the still rankling sores. The Mexican congress, sensing somewhat tardily that it had opened the gates to a horde of ambitious invaders of its territory, ruled that by virtue of the special exclusion clause contained in the charter of the colony no more citizens of North America would be granted entry into Texas. It was powerless, however, to enforce this anathema. The colony had been begun by Americans; their past, present, and especially their future were dependent upon a community of efforts, which in turn required an underlying community of language, customs, and origin. The law was not observed. From this moment on, each new arrival from North America to Texas came not only as a colonist but as a defender of land under attack.

The Mexican government sought to halt the rise of Texas through isolation and division; the Texians reacted very naturally by joining hands tighter than ever and fortifying themselves against impending danger. The decree of May 7, 1824, by which Texas was constituted, said among other declarations that Texas would be "temporarily annexed to the State of Coahuila until its population and resources were large enough to form a separate state." In 1832 Texas was as yet in no position legally to demand the fulfillment of the promise here implied. Despite this truth, it was no less true that the connection of the two states caused Texas considerable trouble and economic losses.

The state of Coahuila was involved most passionately and heatedly in the political agitations of the interior states: all its interest and action were centered upon those endless convulsions which made of Mexico an ever bloodier arena. The interests of Texas were concentrated upon its own survival; its most pressing dangers and most poignant emotions came from its outer limits, where the fierce Indian sought constantly to invade. The colonists in those days could not take a step without holding in one hand their spade, with which to grow crops, and in the other their gun, with which to defend themselves. The soldier-farmers were unaided in this double task by their Latin neighbors, whose attention and thoughts were absorbed elsewhere. As a result, they resolved to demand straightforwardly and simply their separation from Coahuila and the creation of their own distinct and sovereign state. Events took a turn, however, which prevented for some time the sending of their unanimous petition on this subject.

I have noted that the central government had stationed troops in practically every spot in which colonization had occurred. Nacogdoches, San Antonio de Béxar, Goliad, Anáhuac, Galveston, Fort Terán, Victoria, and Tenoxtitlán had garrisons of from thirty to five hundred men. From the frequent contacts between the idle military personnel and the population of working people, conflicts inevitably arose. Strong in their military superiority, the Mexican officers committed numerous acts of violent oppression and unpardonable breaches of authority. Particularly objectionable was the imprisonment of some delegates of the colonists who had been sent on business to the Mexicans. Outraged by this offense, some Texian colonists armed themselves and proceeded to Anáhuac, which was the place of confinement of their fellows. Anáhuac was not heavily garrisoned. Colonel [José de las] Piedras and his detachment were defeated by the Texians, who entered in triumph and released their delegates.

As the colonists returned home still armed and in military order following this expedition, they learned of the so-called Federal insurrection of Santa Anna and the inhabitants of Veracruz against the Central administration of President [Anastasio] Bustamante. Having received nothing but harassment from Bustamante and being somewhat impressed by the liberal policies which Santa Anna promised, they suddenly resolved to support his cause. Having thus resolved, they called upon their fellow citizens to join them in the revolt. Those of Brazoria County had meanwhile begun a revolt by capturing the fort of Velasco. Those of Nacogdoches soon followed suit and drove out their Mexican garrison.

Texas, with the exception of a few strongholds, was almost entirely freed of Mexican troops when the Texians met early in the year 1833 at the Convention of San Felipe and drew up their formal demand for separation from the state of Coahuila. General Austin was elected to deliver this petition in the name of Texas to the national congress. He traveled to Mexico City and did present the request of his fellow citizens. The Mexicans, however, were in a state of such hopeless confusion and unparalleled anarchy that they were unable to heed the supplications of any emissary from without.

Several months elapsed while Austin awaited his answer and observed the lack of attention which his petition received. At last, in a spirit of pity for the quarreling Mexicans and for his own delusions regarding their ability to act, he decided to use deeds rather than words to resolve the question. He wrote to the *ayuntamiento* of Béxar advising the Texians to wait no longer upon a decision from a government unable or unwilling to give one; instead, they should organize themselves immediately into a separate state, by unilateral action. This communication fell into the hands of certain members of the *ayuntamiento* who were loyal to Mexico; they withheld it from their colleagues and informed the central government in Mexico City of it as quickly as they could. Austin meanwhile had left the city. With all his patience exhausted, he had given up his negotiations and had set out for Texas. Orders were issued for his arrest. Six hundred miles away he was captured near Saltillo and brought back to Mexico City, where he was thrown into the prison of the Inquisition and charged with the crime of high treason.

The news of this event caused major repercussions in Texas.

Shortly thereafter, Santa Anna abruptly shifted his allegiance. Having been till then the guiding light of the Federalist Party, he astounded the Mexican people by proclaiming his conversion to the priests' party and his future help to the Centralist government. On May 13, 1834, his henchmen succeeded in dissolving the cabinet and congress. He alone wielded authority, a veritable Cromwell in miniature. Discontent immediately spread like wildfire throughout the country, much more general than ever before.

The state of Coahuila, to which Texas was joined, took a most active part in the revolt. Receiving no support from the Texians, however, it was soon subjugated by the troops of Santa Anna.

From the state of Coahuila, the armed forces proceeded once again into Texas. All hope of peace and self-government vanished from the minds of the settlers. Clashes of interest, ill feeling, and minor uprisings occurred with greater frequency and bitterness than before. Open rebellion broke out in a few isolated spots, the first of which was curiously enough the plain of San Jacinto. Thus fate decreed that both the beginning and end of the struggle between the Anglo-American and the Hispano-Mexican races of Texas were to take place on the same battlefield.

In the month of September, 1835, Stephen F. Austin reappeared upon the scene after an imprisonment of nineteen months in Mexico

City. He instantly became a symbol of patriotism to the American colonists—he was the center of attention. Austin possessed sound judgment. His words exerted great influence on his followers by reason of his strength of character and his candor. The colony was moreover his own achievement; he was its founder and patriarch. During his sojourn and captivity in the very heart of Mexico he had been in a position to assess the weakening effects which internal strife had produced in the nation. He had viewed and touched personally the bleeding wounds of this feeble body. On the other hand, upon his return to Texas he was impressed with the prodigious growth of his young colony. He realized the wealth and patriotic spirit which had developed so vigorously there. Austin's mind was soon made up. On September 8, he addressed his fellow citizens at a meeting in Brazoria with the following words:

The revolution that has spread all over Mexico [has as its object] to change the form of government, destroy the federal constitution of 1824, and establish a central or consolidated Government. The states are to be converted into provinces. . . . Will this act annihilate all the natural rights of Texas, and subject the country to the uncontrolled and unlimited dictation of the new Government? . . . Whether the people of Texas ought or ought not to agree to this change, and relinquish all or part of their constitutional rights . . . is a question of the most vital importance . . . . This matter requires . . . a general consultation of the people.

This declaration, so clearly projecting the orator's opinion across a veil of cautious reserve, settled the matter. From border to border, Texas was on the move to preserve its rights.

In the midst of the general excitement, there reached the colony a military order from General Cos, stationed in Béxar, demanding the immediate arrest and extradition of some Mexican refugees. The Texians refused to honor this order of extradition. The war broke out.

Being named commander in chief, Stephen Austin took charge of seven hundred Texians and marched toward San Antonio de Béxar with the purpose of driving out its garrison. The Mexicans, for their part, marched to Gonzales in order to capture that city, but were forced to withdraw (September, 1835). Another victory for the brave Texians came quickly on the heels of the first. In the month of October the city of Goliad and its fort, one of the strongest of the Mexican military establishments, fell into their hands.

On November 3, an assembly, or general consultation, met at San Felipe as a result of Austin's suggestion to the people. Four days later this body issued a solemn declaration (*solemne declaración*), which announced that Texas was resorting to arms to defend its endangered rights and the principles of the Constitution of 1824 that had been violated; that Texas was no longer either morally or legally bound by its agreement of union; that it did not recognize the authority of the present regime in Mexico, but that it would remain loyal to the Mexican government when and if that nation returned to the constitution and laws under which the colony's ties to Mexico had been formed.

Texas did not yet, it is clear, take a stand for complete independence. By a shrewd yet perfectly honorable political maneuver, it remained committed to the written laws and to its sworn promises. It waited for further violence to shock the civilized world and win sympathy for Texas at the time when the protracted, flagrant violation of justice on the part of its enemy should at last force it to break the remaining ties by which it vainly sought to uphold its promises.

Stephen Austin was elected president of the Consultation. The same assembly named Henry Smith governor of the state and Sam Houston major general of the regular army. The latter, who was to have the glory of saving Texas by the sword and directing it by his sage counsels, was a newcomer in the land. A former state representative [from Tennessee] to the Congress in Washington, he offered his support to the rebels of Texas in answer to the call of adventure and excitement, which his temperament craved. He entered the Texas army as a private; his military knowledge, martial bearing, and dignified manners qualified him for a position of leadership and distinguished him from the rank and file. He became an officer and soon the highest ranking general.

I shall sketch in rapidly the different actions of this first campaign, neglecting the less important ones and concentrating on the major encounters.

The troops that arrived outside Béxar were about to give up the siege for want of sufficient numbers, when one officer of fearless nature and bold intelligence boasted to the troops that he could capture the city if only three hundred determined volunteers would join him. Benjamin Milam was this hero, who more than once led his men to bloody adventure and daring deed. The three hundred readily answered the call and by favor of night set out on the march.

San Antonio de Béxar was protected by a fort, the name of which is inscribed in glorious blood in the annals of Texas: the Alamo. The San Antonio River flowed between the fort and the city, which were joined by two small bridges. Reaching the outskirts of the city at three o'clock in the morning, Milam dispatched a small detachment across the river with orders to simulate an attack on the Alamo with a volley of artillery fire to attract the two garrisons toward this single point. This plan was successful, and he boldly entered the city, which was caught off guard and offered no resistance.

It was not yet settled, however, which of the two sides had in truth been captured by the other. The houses of Béxar were practically all fortified, each of its public squares was well defended, and at the top of an old church were placed cannon that could fire upon any point in the city. It was not until daybreak that the fighting began—deadly, fierce, and stubborn. It lasted five full days, our three hundred Texians the prisoners of their own conquest, surrounded by a hostile populace and obliged to subdue the city house by house, with one assault after another. Running out of supplies and ammunition and being physically exhausted, they made a desperate bayonet attack upon one of the most heavily fortified points of the city, one which overlooked the fort of the Alamo. This position was secured; the three hundred brave men were saved. Yet this victory cost them the life of their leader. Noble Milam, whom Texians have called their Leonidas, had died from a bullet in his head before the hour of triumph.

General Cos, in command at the Alamo, was thunderstruck, and hastened to hoist the white flag of surrender in place of the red-and-black banner which had waved as a signal to the besiegers that they would receive no quarter. Such bombast the Mexicans proffered many a time only to be forced to retract it when their fortunes failed them!

On December 11, 1835, the surrender was signed. The Mexicans still numbered fifteen hundred soldiers; they bowed before troops less than one fifth of their number.

On the fourteenth of the same month, there took place in the city of Tampico a tragic episode of the Mexico-Texas drama, which, even though without consequence on the main course of events, deserves mention at this point.

Wishing to capitalize upon the keen interest that Texas aroused throughout the United States and to use that interest for the Federalist movement, which Texas had espoused, General [José Antonio] Mejía, a Mexican, had gone to New Orleans and enlisted about one hundred young Americans, Frenchmen, Creoles, and Germans. His purpose was to invade Tampico.

At first, everything went smoothly according to his wishes; he could have captured Tampico and who knows how much of Mexico had not his forces dispersed of their own accord. Already, he had the fort and all the artillery of the city proper under his control; already, the civil and military authorities had retreated to a single isolated building and were planning their capitulation. Then Mejía, in an effort to hasten this happy outcome, ordered some thirty of his men to follow him in an attack on the last hideaway of his quaking enemies. "Have you brought us all here only to have us killed?" objected these disobedient soldiers. Mejía retorted, "God! Do you suppose it was to have you dance a jig?" With these words, he seized a hatchet and rushed forth to set a good example to his men. On reaching the door of the fortified building, he turned about and perceived that only one man had followed him. This was a Frenchman. The rest had fled and had dropped their rifles in their flight. Mejía gathered up all the rifles and calmly returned to the fort on the seacoast, where there remained in waiting a nucleus of thirty-five Frenchmen and Louisiana Creoles. This rear guard comprised all the men he had left. During the three days that Mejía and his men continued to occupy the fort, not a single one of the enemy dared to disturb them. While in this retreat, they obtained and equipped a ship, on which they sailed back to New Orleans.

The thirty runaways were arrested by the Mexicans in the woods two days after their rout. They were shot all the more ruthlessly because their enemy was more cowardly than they.

From the Alamo to San Jacinto

BÉXAR, JUNE 5, 1839—The taking of Béxar and the fort of the Alamo by the Texians brought to an end the campaign of 1835. Not a single Mexican soldier remained on Texas territory.

The first months of the year 1836 were taken up with feverish preparations by the Mexicans for a full-scale invasion which would avenge their wounded pride and their recent shame of defeat. For their part, the Texians took steps to obtain means of defense in proportion to the attack; but the disappearance of the enemy left them overconfident: they failed to bring to their task the necessary energy and speed. They went to sleep on their laurels and sought help abroad rather than from their own resources. Agents were sent to the United States to recruit soldiers and collect some money, that prime and indispensable requisite in time of war. New Orleans, always a hotbed of speculation and venturesome schemes, alone supplied a loan of $250,000 (1,250,000 francs) and numerous volunteers. Tennessee and Georgia each promised a battalion.

As the arrival on Texas soil of these tardy reinforcements was anxiously awaited, the question of complete independence and total separation was being debated. Elections were held early in February to name delegates to a General Convention, to meet on March first in the small town of Washington, which had become the seat of government. These elections and the controversial question to be dealt with absorbed the Texians' attention. They laid themselves open to a surprise attack by Santa Anna, who, at the head of 3,000 Mexicans, retook Béxar and pushed its garrison, now reduced to 140 men, to flee for safety within the fort of the Alamo.

The only news that the government of Texas received concerning the critical situation of its troops (it had no others mobilized at the time) was the following letter of Colonel Travis, who commanded the handful of valiant men confined inside the Alamo:

February 24, 1836

Fellow Citizens and Compatriots: I am besieged by a thousand or more of the Mexicans under Santa Anna. I have sustained a continual bombardment and cannonade for twenty-four hours and have not lost a man. The enemy has demanded a surrender at discretion, otherwise the garrison are to be put to the sword, if the fort is taken. I have answered the demand with a cannon shot, and our flag still waves proudly from the walls. I shall never surrender or retreat. Then I call on you in the name of liberty, of patriotism and everything dear to the American character, to come to our aid with all dispatch. The enemy is receiving reinforcements daily and will no doubt increase to three or four thousand in four or five days . . . I am determined to sustain myself as long as possible and die like a soldier who never forgets what is due his own honor and that of his country.

VICTORY OR DEATH!

WILLIAM BARRETT TRAVIS

Burning with the noblest fire of patriotism, this letter expresses what hapless Travis and his friends felt to the end. All perished, and to tell the tale of the bloody incidents of this dreadful tragedy, there lived only one woman and one slave, who escaped the general massacre.

The Negro, Ben,[1] who at the time of the siege was the personal ser-

---

[1] Ben, despite his humble origin and lack of education, is even today considered to be a trustworthy reporter of the siege of the Alamo. Quite obviously, however, his testimony must be accepted with some caution when it is

vant of Santa Anna and who later passed into the possession of General
Houston, has described as follows an interview that occurred in Santa
Anna's lodging between Santa Anna and his aid-de-camp, Colonel
[Juan] Almonte, during the night preceding the capture of the Alamo.
The siege had lasted for twelve days; on the previous day a council of
war had been held, but the Mexican officers had not reached the de-
cision to attack.

Santa Anna ordered that I keep the coffee ready throughout the night [re-
ported the Negro]. Almonte, the aid-de-camp, remained in conference with
him, and they did not go to bed at all. Around midnight, they left the house,
returning between 2:00 and 3:00 A.M. Santa Anna immediately ordered
coffee, and threatened to pierce me through and through with his sword if I
kept him waiting. I served him and noticed Santa Anna looked very much
upset. "This will cost us dearly," said aid-de-camp Almonte. "No matter
how high the cost," replied the general, "it must be done!"

After drinking coffee, they went out and soon I saw rockets ascending in
different directions, and shortly after I heard musketry and cannon, and by
flashes I could distinguish the Mexican troops under the walls of the Alamo.
The report of the cannon, rifles, and musketry was tremendous. It shortly
died away, day broke upon the scene; and Santa Anna and Almonte returned, when the latter remarked: "Another such victory and we are
ruined!" Then they directed me to go with them to the fort, and point out
the bodies of Bowie and Travis,—whom I had before known—which I did.
The sight was most horrid.

---

in direct contradiction to that of the alcalde of San Antonio, José Francisco
Ruiz. Each claims to have been summoned by Santa Anna to identify the bodies
of the Texas leaders; each has a different story regarding the disposal of the
bodies, Ruiz stating that they were burned, Ben that they were buried. For
Ruiz's account, see Louis J. Wortham, *A History of Texas from Wilderness to
Commonwealth,* III, 209–211; for Ben's, see Edward Stiff, *The Texan Emigrant,*
pp. 314–315.

"Ben had previously been a steward on board several American vessels; had
been taken up at New York, in 1835, by Almonte as body servant; had
accompanied him in that capacity to Vera Cruz and thence to Béxar. After the
fall of the Alamo he was sent, with Mrs. Dickerson and Travis' servant, to the
Texan camp at Gonzales, and subsequently became cook to General Houston"
(Chester Newell, *History of the Revolution in Texas,* p. 88).

Another report (the only one in existence besides that of Ben the slave) [2] bears out that the attack took place on the morning of March 6. The Mexicans formed a circle around the fort with their infantry and cavalry to prevent the escape of any Texians. Santa Anna's army was composed of at least 4,000 men, fighting against 140! Santa Anna commanded in person, assisted by four generals and a formidable artillery train. The Texians were worn out from continual attacks and alerts, whether real or false alarms. Nevertheless their morale was never higher than on this momentous day. The enemy twice applied its scaling ladders to the walls of the fort, and twice had to withdraw them. A lull ensued. The Texians were determined, states the witness I quote, to bring to pass the words of their immortal Travis: to render the enemy's victory worse for them than a defeat would be. Spurred on by the commands of Santa Anna and the other officers, the assailants attempted their third attack and were cast down from the walls like sheep. The fight yet continued. Being pressed from all sides, the Texians had no chance to move about nor time to reload their cannon and rifles. They had to defend themselves at last with their rifle butts only, and thus they continued the bloody struggle with hand-to-hand fighting until their strength and lives trickled away through the wounds with which they were covered. All perished. Only one begged for quarter; his inhuman adversaries refused to grant it. The shadows of death closed in upon this scene of extermination and brought it to a halt. "Spirits of the mighty had fallen," continues the narrator of the drama, "but their memory brightens the page of Texan history, and they shall be hailed like the demigods of old . . . as the patterns of virtue!"

This murderous assault lasted less than an hour. Colonel Travis stood on the ramparts, encouraging his men with the cry, "Hurrah, my boys!" up to the moment he himself was shot. As he fell, a Mexican

[2] At this point Gaillardet is guilty of mistranslation of his source (Newell, *History,* p. 89). The latter does *not* imply that no other source was available to him concerning the fall of the Alamo. Having given Ben's evidence, he passes to a second source by the transitional phrase, "On other authority we have it . . ." Gaillardet, confusing the meaning of the preposition *on* and the numeral *one,* interpreted this to mean: "One single other authority do we have."

officer ran upon him and raised his sword for the death blow. Travis, gathering his fast-ebbing strength, struck first, then both fell alike to their death, but "not alike to everlasting fame."[3]

Travis had ordered that Major [Robert] Evans, the artillery commander, set fire to the ammunition at the last possible moment, so that the enemy, as well as they themselves, should explode together. Luckily for Santa Anna, the Major was killed at the moment he was about to apply the flame to the gun powder. Santa Anna was so shaken and enraged that he drew forth his knife and twice buried it in the corpse of the enemy officer who had almost destroyed him.

The bodies of the Texians were declared heretical and denied a burial: the Mexicans piled them up and burned them. Among the victims of this fatal day was the heroic figure David Crockett, of Tennessee, the great Western trapper whose marvelous adventures have become popular American legends and are retold for the entertainment of all in every saloon of cities large and small. The bodies of his companions formed a circle around him. James Bowie, whose trusty knife has become the model of the favorite weapon of the Western frontiersman, was confined to a sickbed when the Mexicans stormed the fort. As it came Bowie's turn to be transported to the pyre, General Cos stopped the bearers of his body and exclaimed, "This was too brave a man to be burned like a dog!" Then he added, "But no matter; throw him on! [*¡Pues no es cosa, echad!*]"

As this awful tragedy thus resolved itself behind the walls of the Alamo, an even bloodier episode, and one even more shameful for the name of Santa Anna, was taking place on the plains of Goliad.

Colonel [James] Fannin, of Texas, with a mere five hundred men

---

[3] Gaillardet here translates directly from Newell, as also in the course of the previous paragraph (Newell, *History,* p. 90). Even when quotation marks are not used, the entire account of the siege is nothing more than a translation from Newell. The second witness, after Ben, would appear to be Travis's slave, Joe, who uses the comparison "like sheep" in describing the Mexicans pouring over the walls, and who is responsible for the traditional account of Travis's death. Cf. Amelia W. Williams, "A Critical Study of the Siege of the Alamo," *Southwestern Historical Quarterly,* XXXVII (April, 1934), 42.

under his command had been threatened with a siege by a division of the Mexican army under [José] Urrea. This division had appeared unexpectedly outside of Goliad. As the two sides were too unequally matched, Fannin ordered an evacuation of the city before the enemy could reach it. The retreat was in progress, but luck was against him, for he came face to face with the troops he was attempting to evade. He had left behind the only cannon he possessed. The battle cost many lives and lasted till nightfall. The Texians, who had run out of their small supply of ammunition, hoped to slip away under cover of night. However, a Mexican agent appeared to offer them honorable terms of surrender. According to the offer, Fannin and his men would be treated as prisoners of war. Those of his soldiers who were citizens of the United States would be returned to New Orleans at the expense of the Mexican government; the Texians would be exchanged for an equal number of Mexican prisoners. The two commanders affixed their signatures to the treaty, and the Texians surrendered their weapons. Urrea had the prisoners led to Goliad and a copy of the treaty sent to Santa Anna at Béxar. The latter called a meeting of his officers, which was held in strict privacy and was marked by a very heated debate. Santa Anna concluded it by rising and repeating from his doorsill the words: "*¡Sí, sí, sí!*" The inhabitants of Béxar were to learn only later the import of these words.

On March 17, following the courier's return from Santa Anna to Urrea, the prisoners of Goliad were led forth from the city; the Americans were separated from the Texians, as though each group were to take the direction set down in the treaty. Each group was then divided into three parts and lined up in single file. Each line was faced by a double row of soldiers armed with musket and bayonet. When this was done, the poor prisoners realized what lay in store for them. Soon the order to halt was uttered in clipped tone by the officers. All motion ceased; all voices fell silent. The signal was given; all the victims fell, in mute resignation to one of the most treacherous acts of deceit which has ever blemished the pages of history.

Colonel Fannin was confined to his bed by a wound when his compatriots were led to their *butchery*, to use the word of a Texas writer as he graphically described the events. After the massacre a messenger was sent to him to inform him that he too must prepare for death. "Tell them I am prepared," he replied. His only request to his executioners was that they should try not to shoot him in the head. When he reached the place of execution he pushed away the soldier who, with trembling hands, was about to tie a handkerchief around his eyes; he snatched the handkerchief, tied it on his head himself, bared his breast, and fell down lifeless.

These repeated defeats finally aroused the people of Texas from the lethargy in which they had been plunged by reason of a few months of peace and quiet. Patriotic zeal, which had ebbed all too seriously, now rallied and grew intense in response to the cry of the fallen martyrs. An army was assembled and equipped, which, though small in number, was formidable in courage. The Convention which met on March 2, 1836, enthusiastically voted in favor of the declaration of complete independence. The new [*ad interim*] government was entrusted to the following executives: David G. Burnet, president; Lorenzo de Zavala, vice-president; and Samuel Houston, commander in chief.

Santa Anna sent to the latter a courier with an offer of peace and general amnesty if the Texians would lay down their arms and submit to government by Mexico. Houston's answer was short and to the point: "Dear Sir, You have succeeded in killing some of our brave fighters, but the Texians are not whipped yet."

The Texas army was then on the banks of the Colorado River. It was as yet composed of just fourteen hundred men; however, these men were burning with desire to encounter the enemy. Houston took advantage of this enthusiasm by leading them toward the Brazos to capture San Felipe, then heading toward Donahoe's, after sending an order to the volunteers from the United States to stop their advance to meet him, and instead to take a stand on the banks of the Trinity River. Having reached Donahoe's he was undecided whether to continue in the direction of Nacogdoches or Harrisburg. A lucky incident enabled him to make up his mind. A Mexican courier was arrested, and from the dispatches and documents found in his possession, Houston learned that Santa Anna's objectives were the seizure of the small towns of Harrisburg and New Washington,[4] and that he considered the war practically at an end, as he confidently advanced across the state, unaware of the size or position of the Texas army. He had already burned the first of these two towns and, following this exploit, was going down in the direction of Lynch's Ferry on the San Jacinto, at the head of only one of the three divisions which composed his army. The opportunity was splendid; Houston realized the possibilities.

He immediately set out to overtake Santa Anna, crossed the river which lay between them, and, leaving the sick and the provisions behind, chose a camp on the western side of Buffalo Bayou on the morning of April 19, at about half-a-mile's distance from the confluence of this small stream with the larger San Jacinto River.

On the twentieth he took a position at the edge of a wood beside the Bayou. He had the wood to the rear and faced an open plain dotted with small clumps of trees.

Santa Anna soon appeared. He was greeted with an unexpected dis-

---

[4] Nowhere more clearly than in this passage does Gaillardet display his bias in favor of Texas against Mexico. Departing from Newell, he briefly describes Sam Houston's retreat to the east, accompanied by a disgruntled and deserting army, as though it were a triumphal march from victory to victory at the head of a loyal and enthusiastic soldiery.

"Donahoe's" refers to a farm owned by a certain Donahoe near Hempstead. "It was at Donoho's [sic] that the road from Groce's to Harrisburg crossed that from San Felipe to eastern Texas" (Henderson K. Yoakum, *A History of Texas from Its First Settlement in 1685 to Its Annexation to the United States in 1846*, II, 122).

New Washington was the town on Galveston Bay, not to be confused with Washington-on-the-Brazos; it is the present Morgan's Point, and was in fact burned by Santa Anna. For an account of a visit to the charred ruins and of James Morgan's reminiscences of the passing of Santa Anna's troops, see *Texas in 1837: An Anonymous, Contemporary Narrative*, ed. Andrew Forest Muir, pp. 13–17.

The interception of the Mexican courier was one of many valuable services rendered Houston by his trusty scout, Erastus "Deaf" Smith (cf. William Kennedy, *Texas: The Rise, Progress, and Prospects of the Republic of Texas*, p. 586).

charge of Texian artillery. He withdrew and placed his infantry in a grove of trees located to the left of the Texian encampment and about a quarter of a mile away. The day passed with an exchange of skirmishes, in which the Texians came out on top; this was good for their morale.

The next day five hundred men under the command of General Cos arrived to reinforce Santa Anna's forces. Houston decided that he should not put off any longer the attack which was to settle once and for all the fate of Texas. Further delay would mean risking the arrival of all the rest of the Mexican army to further weigh against the Texian troops, who were already outnumbered by Santa Anna's present force.

A bridge over Sims Bayou was the only means of retreat which lay open to the Mexicans. Houston's first command was therefore that it be destroyed. At 3:30 P.M. his army set out for the attack: divided into three groups, it marched in unbroken silence—not a drum, not a bugle, not a voice! A historian of Texas states that everyone was rousing his soul for the conflict.[5] When they had approached within a short distance of the enemy, the single command of "Fire!" was heard through the ranks; a general discharge wrought death and disorder in the camp of the unsuspecting Mexicans. Then the war cry rang out: "Charge! Remember the Alamo!" cried General Houston. "Remember the Alamo!" repeated the soldiers, and they charged with their bayonets, their vociferations mingling with the sound of artillery fire and the savage strains of the patriotic song, "Yankee Doodle."[6] This was more

---

[5] The phrase is taken from Newell, *History*, p. 107.

[6] Whether "Yankee Doodle" was actually played as a stimulus to the charge is a question open to debate. Early histories offer conflicting evidence, some contending that "Will You Come to the Bower?" served this purpose. Gaillardet gets his information from Newell: "'Yankee Doodle' was heard above the roar of arms; and, with the shout of 'the Alamo,' they rushed upon their foe,— and victory rewarded their valor, and vengeance atoned for their wrongs" (Newell, *History*, pp. 107–108). Besides, Gaillardet had heard the tune during an anniversary celebration, as he has already reported (Chapter One). Stiff reports ". . . an attack to the tune of 'Come to the Bower'" (*Texan Emigrant*, p. 103), but later contradicts himself with the statement, "The soul-stirring notes of 'Yankee Doodle' proclaimed a charge, and with irresistible tempestuosity

than a battle: it was a slaughter. The Texians were athirst for vengeance; the Mexicans fled in terror.

The conflict lasted about eighteen minutes [one reads in General Houston's official report], until we were in possession of the enemy's encampment, colours, all their camp stores and baggage . . . . The rout commenced at half-past four and the pursuit continued until twilight . . . . The enemy's loss was 630 killed, wounded 208 . . . prisoners 730. President General Santa Anna . . . was not taken until the twenty-second, and General Cos yesterday, the twenty-fourth. In the battle, our loss was two killed and twenty-three wounded.

Santa Anna was not the last to take flight in the general exodus of his army. A Texian officer[7] relates that on the day following the battle thirty men were sent out to look for fugitives. While they were halted in a field beside a creek, which is one of the branches of Buffalo Bayou:

. . . they espied a Mexican, bending his course towards the bridge. He stopped a moment to gaze around him and then started on. They rode up to where he was. As soon as he saw them, he laid [sic] down in the grass, which was high enough to hide him from their view. When they arrived at the spot, he was lying on his side, with a blanket over his head. They called him to rise, when he only took the blanket from his face. They called to him a second time and a third, to get up; whereupon he rose and stood for a moment, and, finding himself surrounded, advanced towards them and desired to shake hands; whereupon one immediately offered him his hand. He pressed and kissed it. He then offered them as a bribe a splendid watch, ex-

---

they rushed upon the Mexicans" (p. 324). Kennedy's *Texas,* p. 593, mentions only "Will You Come to the Bower I have Shaded for You?" which, he implies, Houston ordered played as an ironical joke comparable to that of the familiar nursery rhyme, "'Will you come into my parlor?' said the spider to the fly." Popular tradition sides with the latter: the song, with words attributed to Thomas Moore, was published in a Centennial Edition (Boston, 1936) which states: "The music of this song was played by a small band of musicians during the battle of San Jacinto. . . . It is therefore known as the national song of the Republic of Texas."

[7] The officer was James A. Sylvester, a sergeant, according to Yoakum's *History,* II, 147. It is evident that Gaillardet borrows the relation from Newell; the latter does not state the name of the officer (Newell, *History,* pp. 195–196).

ceedingly valuable jewelry, and a large sum of money, which . . . they refused. He then asked them where their brave Houston was. They replied he
was in camp. Through one of the party acting as interpreter,[8] they asked him
who he was. He replied a private soldier; when one observing the bosom of
his shirt, which was very splendid, he directed his attention to it. He immediately said that he was an aid to Santa Anna, and burst into a flood of tears.
He was told in a mild tone not to grieve, he should not be hurt. He was
dressed in common clothes, had no arms,[9] and appeared dejected, complain-
ing of pains in the breast and of not being able to walk. They proceeded with
him for two or three miles, which he rode. He then dismounted and walked
into camp . . . .

When conducted into the tent of General Houston, Santa Anna addressed
him as follows: "Soy Antonio López de Santa Anna, Presidente de la Re-
pública Mexicana y General-en-Jefe del Ejército de Operaciones."

General Houston, for his part, has supplied the following account of
his interview with Santa Anna:[10]

I was lying on a blanket at the root of a tree, with my saddle for a pillow,
when Santa Anna approached my tent, studiously inquiring for Houston. I
was in a partial slumber and lying, for the sake of an easy position for my
wounded ankle, upon my left side, with my face turned from Santa Anna as
he approached. The first I knew of Santa Anna's presence was by a squeeze
of the hand and the calling of my name; whereupon I looked upon him with
a mild expression of countenance, which seemed to inspire him with confidence and hope of life, which evidently he had expected to forfeit. I desired
him to be seated upon a medicine chest standing by, upon which accordingly

[8] Lorenzo de Zavala, Jr., son of the *interim* vice-president of the Republic,
served as interpreter on this occasion (Gustav Dresel, *Houston Journal: Adventures in North America and Texas, 1837–1841,* p. 133).

[9] "Santa Anna's sword was found on the ground of the San Jacinto Battleground, but stripped of its hilt which, according to him, was worth more than
$7,000 (35,000 francs)" (GN).

[10] Newell reports Houston's words in the third person; Gaillardet reverted to
the first person in translating this report into French. Accordingly, our present
version in English uses the words of Newell changed to the first person, as
though Houston were speaking them. The account was based upon an interview
that Newell had with Houston, but did not purport to reproduce Houston's
exact words.

he sat down, much agitated, with his hands pressed against his chest. Presently, he asked for opium, which being given him, he swallowed a considerable quantity, and soon became more composed. He said to me, "General, you were born, like Wellington, to no ordinary destiny; you have conquered the Napoleon of the West." He soon desired to know what disposal was to be made of him. Waiving the question, I told him he must order all the Mexican troops in Texas to march beyond the Río Grande, and then spoke of his late cruelty to the Texans, and first at the Alamo; upon which he said that at the Alamo he had acted according to the laws of war of all nations. I then spoke of the massacre of Fannin and his men . . . upon which he proceeded to say that their executions were in obedience to the orders of the Mexican government. "You are that government," I retorted.

Changing the subject in order to return to the point which concerned and tormented him the most, he told me that if the Texans would spare his life, he would repay them by the greatest services, in particular by recognizing their independence. "How can you make that commitment?" I asked. "Recognition of Texas can only be granted by an official act of your government." "Why, my dear friend," he fatuously exclaimed, "that government is myself." "That is exactly what I was trying to say a moment ago concerning the massacre of Goliad!" He turned pale and stammered a few words in an embarrassed attempt to draw a distinction between the two situations.[11] Upon this subject, the conversation was waived, and, it being night, I asked him if he would have my camp bed, which being desired, I ordered it to be brought into his tent. He reclined upon it, but did not sleep during the night, being in constant dread of assassination.

What was to become of Santa Anna became the burning issue of the day. The entire army was still aroused with anger over the cruelties at Goliad and the Alamo. It demanded that the bloodthirsty general be

---

[11] The paragraph thus far is an interpolation, not found in Newell's account of his interview with Houston. We translate therefore directly from the French of Gaillardet, from the beginning of the paragraph down to the sentence containing the words, "Upon this subject, the conversation was waived . . ." Presumably, the dramatist Gaillardet invented a bit of dialogue to provoke a laugh at the expense of the defeated dictator; the historian Gaillardet temporarily withdrew. The history of Texas is such a complicated tissue of truth and legend, the two elements being so inextricably interwoven, that one more strand of embroidery cannot be regarded amiss.

offered in sacrifice to the shades of his victims. Samuel Houston and some other leaders, more mindful of the best interests than of the emotions of their country, however justifiable the latter might be, were agreed to pursue a more merciful course. One group favored a sacrifice to the past; the other, a sacrifice to the future. The divisions of the Mexican army which remained under orders of Generals Urrea and [Vicente] Filisola still totaled more than five thousand men. This was three times the size of the Texian forces. Doubtless their recent victory greatly increased the prestige and morale of the Texians, while it weakened their adversaries correspondingly; nevertheless, the struggle could still be terrible and the outcome in doubt if an executed Santa Anna should bequeath to his followers the task of avenging him and should teach them, by his death, that they could expect no mercy from their relentless enemies. In such a conjuncture, was it not wiser to use the weakness and terrors of Santa Anna as a means of driving a good bargain? He seemed prepared to sacrifice his honor. His orders would probably be carried out by an army which still regarded him as its commander in chief; likewise, his pledges might perhaps be respected by a government of which he was the chief executive.

The latter reasoning at length prevailed in the cabinet. As a result, a treaty was signed with Santa Anna, who ordered Generals Urrea and Filisola to evacuate Texas and to exchange their prisoners; he promised that he would never again wage war against Texas and that he would use his influence not only to prevent another outbreak of hostilities but also to bring about the recognition by the Mexican congress of the independence of Texas. Thus, Santa Anna, a dishonorable citizen and a dishonorable general, sacrificed to his own cowardice the interests of his country and threw away from it, as much as it was in his power to do so, one of the richest provinces that made up his domain!

Happenings in the New Republic

SAN FELIPE, JUNE 30, 1839—Houston, the victor of San Jacinto, was elected president of the Texas Republic in September, 1836, and [in October] the Congress met in Columbia.

This Congress had a large order of business to deal with. Administration, justice, finance, the army itself were all either to be established or reorganized. For the social edifice which was to rise, there existed as yet only the site which victory had won and the plans which the Constitution had laid down. This Constitution was adopted on March 17, 1836, when the massacres of Goliad and the Alamo were all too fresh in the people's minds. It was to be the basis for all civil and political laws of Texas; therefore, its chief provisions must be presented here. I shall attempt to make as brief a summary as possible.

CONSTITUTION OF TEXAS

Three powers: executive, legislative, and judicial.

A president, a House of Representatives, and a Senate.

The president is elected by the vote of the citizens for a three-year term and is ineligible the following term.

He must be thirty-five years of age and a resident of Texas for at least three years before election.

He has the right of pardon, makes treaties subject to ratification by a two-thirds vote of the Senate, and appoints all officeholders that are not specifically mentioned in the Constitution.

The president receives a salary of $10,000, the vice-president $3,000, cabinet members $3,000.

The term for representatives is one year.

They must be twenty-five years old and citizens of the Republic, having resided in their city or district for six months prior to election.

The term for senators is three years. They must be thirty years old and residents of their district for at least one year.

One third of the Senate is elected annually.

Senators and representatives receive remuneration for time spent in session.

Number of representatives: forty.

Number of senators: one half the number of representatives.

Each law must be passed by the two Houses and approved by the president, who must make his decision within five days. If he vetoes a bill, a vote of two thirds of both Houses is required to overrule him.

Any citizen aged twenty-one years and a resident for six months in the country has the right to vote.

No paid public official is eligible [for a seat in the Congress].

Judges are elected for four years, are eligible for re-election, and are paid.[1]

Any accused person may be freed from imprisonment upon payment of sufficient bail, except when under charge of capital offense.

No person may be imprisoned for debts.

No foreigner may own lands, unless by title issued directly by the government.

Freedom of the press is guaranteed, with the admonition not to abuse it.

The jury system, *habeas corpus*, and common law of England are the temporary bases of civil and criminal law.

The purest radicalism clearly dictated this Constitution, some defects of which were quick to appear in practice. For instance, the necessity of holding annual elections stirred the minds of many with the strong-

---

[1] They were "elected by joint ballot of both houses of Congress" (Louis J. Wortham, *A History of Texas from Wilderness to Commonwealth*, III, 420).

est desire for an amendment which would relieve them of this immoderate exercise of the right to vote. Likewise, the prohibition of ownership that affects all foreigners, a policy derived from the disastrous old Spanish colonial system, has proved detrimental to the development of local agriculture and industry. Foreign capitalists have kept a tight grip on their kindly feelings and their purse strings in a country which bars them from property rights. It is urgent that Texas revise these unsound, foolish provisions, both on paper and in practice. Its future depends on its doing so.

The truth of the matter is that when the Texians adopted this hastily-thrown-together Constitution, they thought of it more as the symbol of their independence than as the creed of their nationality. Indeed, no sooner had this independence been proclaimed than the new nation, a hesitant satellite in its liberty, gravitated toward a planetary center and sought a place among the twenty-four stars of the American sky, with which it felt the kinship of birth, language, and customs. By almost unanimous vote, the population of Texas declared itself desirous "of being joined to the great political family of the north."

In response to this expression of public opinion, the President sent an emissary to Washington to obtain, first of all, recognition of Texas independence; this first step, if successful, was to be followed by an offer to become a part of the United States without delay.

The Washington cabinet granted the desired recognition,[2] but, for political reasons, partly tactical and partly beyond their control, they refused to annex the land and people which offered themselves. Farther on, I shall attempt to explain this refusal. This land was unquestionably an object of their covetousness! These people were surely children who had been born and reared on their soil! This turn of events caused a sensation in European political circles and a still greater one in Texas. Disowned by the family by whom it had sought to be adopted,

---

[2] This statement is incorrect. Recognition was obtained in the last hours of Jackson's administration by congressional action, not that of the Cabinet. Winning congressional authorization, the President appointed Alcée LaBranche as chargé d'affaires to the Republic (Wortham, *History*, III, 399–406).

Texas had to make up its mind to start its own independent family. Its petition to become a state had been denied; it therefore undertook to become a nation and to rely entirely upon its own resources.

A capital became necessary for the sovereign state of Texas. Several existing cities vied for this honor; the Texians preferred, however, to seize this occasion to build a new city.

Into Galveston Bay flows the stream called Buffalo Bayou. This stream is narrow, its course meanders, but it is deep, and it penetrates into the heart of a vast, important region, for which it provides a valuable outlet. On this bayou, at the farthest inland point that is navigable, the government established its official seat, toward the close of the year 1837. The future capital was named Houston, after the victor of San Jacinto who was then president of the Republic.

When the members of the government and of the two legislatures arrived at the designated site, they found two cabins there, dignified with the title of houses, and a total population of a dozen souls. They set to work, and soon a large wooden barn arose to join the first two houses. This barn received the majestic name of Capitol. The interior was divided in two, by means of a partition of planks. The Senate was established on one side, the House of Representatives on the other. At night the cold was quite bitter, and neither the president nor the cabinet members, nor the senators, nor the representatives had a single bed on which to lie; they filled great canvas bags with wood shavings; president, cabinet members, senators and representatives each crawled into his bag. This mode of existence continued for several weeks.[3]

Today, Houston has a resident population of more than two thousand, which, swelled by the influx of transients and foreigners, sometimes reaches four thousand. More than four hundred houses have been built, and hundreds more are seen to be under construction nearby. Property taxes in this thriving community already amount to

[3] Saligny also marveled at the legislators who built their own Capitol and then slept in it under the most primitive conditions. His description, paralleling that of Gaillardet, is contained in his report of June 24, 1839, to the French government (quoted by Mary Katherine Chase, *Négociations de la République du Texas en Europe, 1837–1845,* p. 34, note 3).

$2,405,865 (nearly thirteen million francs). Two theaters, with American actors who have come from the north of the United States, give regular nightly performances. Six or seven steamboats maintain constant communication between the port of Houston and that of Galveston, as also with the cities on the Trinity River. The mere sight of the busy steamboat navigation is enough to instruct the foreigner, as he sets foot upon this soil, as to the kind of people he will meet here. The channel of Buffalo Bayou is so narrow and the steamboats which ply its waters are so hemmed in between its two banks that the trees growing close to the water tear into the hulls of the plucky crafts and sweep their decks of anything which has been rashly left lying on them. A steamboat never arrives at Houston without having left along the way a few portions of its stern rail, or who knows? Perhaps even a passenger! It arrives, however, and that is all that an American insists upon. A railroad which is to connect Houston with the shores of the Brazos and Colorado Rivers was recently voted by the legislature, and the financing of it has been almost fully underwritten by investors. Lastly, the vicinity of Houston possesses some steam sawmills along with its numerous dwellings. A city and an entire region have sprung into life there, and have no sooner sprung than they have mushroomed amazingly.

Once the wheels were in motion and the future of the city and region had become assured, the politicians of Texas soon set their sights farther afield. The dream of another capital seized them, and they determined that this one, like the previous one, should be built by themselves and to their own specifications. Houston is not a central point: it is located on the banks of a secondary stream and in a comparatively infertile region, whereas the Brazos and Colorado Rivers, the two great arteries of Texas, flow through the heart of the country, water the richest land, and yet have remained devoid of any large cities. In addition to the basically geographic reasons which led the Texas legislature to vote for a removal, a political motive existed which continues to be a prime consideration to this race of hardy pioneers. For them, the plan of a new capital was at the same time a plan for a future campaign against the Indians, who constitute the only remaining hostile element against Texas. At this point, I must say a word about the Indians.

The most dreadful are the Comanches, whose tribe occupies the lands to the north and northeast of San Antonio de Béxar. Their population is estimated to include no less than fifty thousand braves. They have numerous villages, located in the more fertile parts and on sites of scenic beauty chosen for their defensibility against attack from without. In them their councils are held, and there they leave their wives, the elderly, and their young under protection of a sufficient guard, while they roam on their far-flung, bold forays.

The Comanches are almost always on horseback. The horse is their lifelong companion—they are born with him in common liberty, roam the woods with him, feed themselves with the same fruits of the earth as he, and often die a common death with him. The Mexicans, and after them the Texians, have pursued with equal zeal both the savages and their savage steeds. The animals, known by their Indian name of *mustang*, often appear in herds numbering a thousand or twelve hundred. They are small, have thick short coats, legs like deer, narrow heads, and fierce eyes. They are generally quite undersized and of a somewhat delicate constitution. They are not native to the country, but are degenerate descendants of the first Spanish breeds imported to Mexico. They are caught by means of a lasso, which circles their necks and then binds them so painfully that they remember the experience for the rest of their lives. If, after an escape, the poor creatures feel this fatal noose a second time around them, they instantly come to a halt, afraid to take another step. Once captured, they are turned over to the guard of two of their fellow horses who, by the corrupting education of servitude, have been trained to hunt their free brothers untiringly and then also to become their vigilant, intelligent keepers. Texians keep no pastures or stables for these animals; they mark them with their branding iron and leave them on the open plains. They send out their home slaves, the Negroes, to retrieve these prairie slaves whenever they want to use them.

The Comanches use bows and arrows, as do the other Indian tribes, but as an additional weapon they carry a long lance with an iron point attached to one of its ends. In battle their braves are preceded by two of their women, or *squaws,* who serve as trumpeters, one might say. These women, by varying the pitch of their loud, strident voices, convey to the fighting troops whatever commands the chiefs issue for an advance, retreat, or other movement. When the Comanches make an attack their standard tactic is almost invariably to rush forward in a closed rank as quick as a flash; then, having reached a certain point, to separate abruptly into two squadrons, one darting to the left, the other to the right, in order to surround the enemy.

These people, who in their nomadic existence share many features with the Arabs of the deserts, will exhibit to you, just as the Arabs will, the two outstanding virtues of faithfulness and hospitality, provided only that you are not to be classed among their enemies. If you are, they will show you no pity. The Mexicans long experienced the truth of this observation, and so the name of Comanche became with them a term of horror and bloody insult. The Americans, on the other hand, during the early days of their penetration of Louisiana and Texas, received only the kindest treatment from these savages, who did not yet take them to be the despoilers of their ancestral lands.

The powerful tribe of Comanches are today the only remaining representatives and fierce defenders of the old Indian nationality, which has been crushed and dispersed across Mexican and Texian territory. In addition, I must mention the tribes of Waccos, Leppans, Eushanees, Tankoways, and a few others who are nothing more than weak, disunified remnants.[4] The famous anthropophagous tribe of Caranka-

---

[4] Despite the unorthodox spellings, these names may be identified as the Wacos, Lipan Apaches, Hasinai, and Tonkawas, respectively; the tribe mentioned in the conclusion of the paragraph is today spelled Karankawa. The only questionable one is the Eushanees: Gaillardet's spelling suggests a possible identification with the Yskanis (other recorded spellings of the same are Yxcanis and Ascanis). However, as the latter are thought to have been an earlier name for the Wacos, with whom they form an identical culture, we prefer to think that Gaillardet refers to the Hasinai. The Hasinai confederacy was an East Texas group of Caddo tribes, members of the southeast culture area and akin to the Natchez. If this interpretation is the correct one, Gaillardet

huays, who dwelt along the shores of the Gulf of Mexico and maintained a defense against the Spaniards, are reduced to 108 braves, the last survivors of the general massacre of this once-dreaded race. They obtained mercy from General Austin only by seeking asylum in a church of the city of La Bahía and by promising to lead peaceful lives within the confines of a small reservation of which the Lavaca River would form an impassable boundary. They have kept their word and have become harmless enough as savages go, and, if one is to believe them, dreadfully sorry about their past weakness for human flesh, of which failing they are entirely cured.

In its beginnings, the American colony of Texas scarcely had any warfare to wage with the Indians, except for the Carankahuays, whom I have just mentioned. The Americans had first to take Texas away from Mexico before picking any quarrel with the Indians. Therefore, the Comanches themselves, their touchiest neighbors, regarded the Texians for quite a while as allies rather than enemies. Once Texas was independent and its hands were free of the grip which had absorbed its every effort, it lost no time in spreading northward to the fertile plains that the savages occupied. Eager farmers longingly eyed these richly endowed regions that only the barren tent of the savage had heretofore touched. The leaders of Texas divided these lands into tracts long before they had anything but the dream of authority over them; the dubious possessions were put on the market; it was easy enough to buy them, but a different matter to actually occupy them. The Comanches had leaped into action upon their horses, had seized their lances, and were determined to defend to the last ditch the prairies that formed the patrimony of their warring, wandering existence. Soon they could not restrict themselves to defense and were launching of-

has included, among the tribes he lists, three of the four basic cultural types as classified by twentieth-century archeology: Western Gulf (Karankawa), Plains tribes in successive waves (Lipan, Waco, Tonkawa, Comanche), and Southeast (Hasinai); only the Puebloan Jumanos are omitted, and rightly so: they inhabited the Río Grande Valley, which Gaillardet regarded as still part of Mexico. Cf. W. W. Newcomb, Jr., *The Indians of Texas: From Prehistoric to Modern Times,* pp. 21–25.

fensive attacks. Many caravans fell victim to their fury; many homes became the scenes of their bloody revenge. The city of Béxar itself, the oldest city in Texas, guarded by its fort looking out to the wilderness on the northwest, has sometimes suffered from the Comanches, whose raids have led them to face death in the heart of the city.

How did the Texian government react to this situation?

It reasoned that the only great advantage of the savages was the distance that separated their strongholds from the civilized communities; therefore, it recommended that the seat of government be moved to the frontier, that is, almost to the heart of the enemy territory. By this bold tactic, enthusiastically voted in the most recent legislative session, the leaders challenge their fellow citizens who are as yet unsettled and scattered to follow them if they love their country. A large segment of the population will follow in battle array; they are already girding themselves for action. The Indians inevitably will be forced back into the wilderness, and Texas will win a capital and one more province to boot. This policy smacks of the ancient Romans. It is undeniable that the government, to do this, possesses both wisdom and courage to a high degree.

Already the location has been selected on which the new capital is to be built. It is to be on the banks of the Brazos River [sic] in Bastrop County. Its original name was Waterloo; the Texian government has removed that name and rechristened it Austin, after the patriarch of Texas. Moreover, it is a rich and delightful location. Copper mines are near at hand, from which I have seen magnificent specimens. Marble and other stone quarries, not generally found elsewhere in the country, are there to furnish the Texians with building materials for a capital worthy of the name.

Houston, the present capital, is alone fretting at the impending move. It will be bereft of its present grandeur. Foreboding its abandonment, the city seeks to retain the elusive gods within its sanctuary. The new capital is, however, one of President Lamar's most cherished dreams, and nothing will make him give it up. The President is the shrewd executor and faithful servant of the law. He has informed his cabinet and employees that when the time comes he would, if need be, journey alone to the spot where the law has decreed that he should bear the home and seals of the state.

President Mirabeau Buonaparte Lamar is a man of few words, but a man of action. The Texians call him *the dumb President,* because of his extraordinary reluctance to speak. This paucity of words is the result of his dreamy, reflective personality and of a certain natural difficulty which he experiences is expressing himself. One subject can cause the President to open up with obvious pleasure and can produce a flow of voluble, expansive discourse: this is the war with Mexico. On this topic, his tongue loses all restraints, and he becomes a forceful, spirited, rapid talker.

President Lamar is of old French stock and has the warmest regard for the land which cradled his forebears. As the cavalry commander at the battle of San Jacinto, he received the highest commendation in the official account of his victory as published by the commander in chief, General Houston, whom he later succeeded as president. Apart from their bravery and military aptitude, the two men who have been chosen to guide the destinies of an independent Texas could not be more dissimilar.

Samuel Houston was as free of his words and speeches as his successor is guarded in his. He was a facile speaker who enjoyed being heard and hearing himself talk; Mirabeau Lamar is unpretentious, and cloaks his keen judgment within an almost childlike timidity and restraint. The only exterior idiosyncracy he has adopted is to generally wear his coat buttoned high up his frame, topped by his shirt collar, which flaps down at right angles over his tie. The peculiarities that Samuel Houston affected in his attire taxed one's credulity. The ex-President is a magnificently built man. Tall, erect, graceful and manly in his proportions, he bears the head of Antinoüs upon the neck of a Circassian maid. This strange man loves adventure, and is completely fearless and immensely self-centered. His ideas are always original and often wild. This accounts for his long sojourn among the American Indians. Eager to explore the unknown, sensitive to every impulse, possessed of wanderlust, he threw himself into a savage milieu, soon took a liking to it, and ended up wedded to it, to a certain extent. When he came back to American life he had acquired numerous traits of his former hosts, which he did not shed; he was a curious mixture of the perfect gentleman and the Choctaw. He shared the Indians' fondness for the gaudy, their propensity for physical intemperance and moral vanities. He possessed their stormy instincts and also their clairvoyance and natural inspiration: their strengths and their weaknesses. His favorite costume, which we describe next, is supplied as indicative of his character.

His hair was powdered in a grotesque way of his own invention; he always went about with his neck bare; a broad collar falling from the top of his shirt was retained only by a pink or blue ribbon, the loops of which dangled loosely on his chest. He invariably wore boots with the tops folded down to reveal a red, yellow, green, or other brightly colored lining. Lastly, the most beautiful item of his attire was a velvet waistcoat that he had ordered from Paris. It was covered with gold embroidery worth twelve hundred francs. This vest was his pride and joy.

His manners were, on the other hand, quite aristocratic, very smooth and cordial. His mind was keen, quick, and rather witty, but defenseless against flattery. With this weapon, it is said, the prisoner Santa Anna managed gradually to sooth and win over the one who with a single gesture could have snuffed out his life. The Yankee Americans accused Houston of being one to whom nothing was sacred. The Southerners, who are less fanatical in their devotion to human and divine law, were content to call him *a smart man*.

As a matter of fact, this accusation of immorality which Northern puritanism directed against the former president of Texas actually encompassed at the time the entire population. The young nation and the old leader were alike included in the anathema.[5] The girls from the north of the continent obstinately refused to consider matrimonial

[5] Samuel Houston (1793–1863) was in his forty-third year when he became president of the Republic. Bowie, Travis, Fannin, Rusk, and Lamar were

proposals from their pioneer menfolk who had become the citizens of
this new Rome in the making. Texas found itself forced to consider
another rape of the Sabine women. Fortunately, the American women
came around to a more reasonable and humane viewpoint. Today, no
barrier exists between the two populations of like origin and language.
The female sex is still far in the minority in Texas. Houston, the temporary capital, has only 453 women out of a total population usually
hovering around 3,000.

One of the principal tasks of President Lamar has been to whitewash his country of the accusations that have tarnished it in the eyes
of the world. Naturally inclined toward a firm hand in government, he
realized that firmness was a prime need of a new state in which mores
and discipline were in their infancy. As a result, since his term of
office began, Texas has become one of the most secure places in America, with respect to the property, liberty, and life of its citizens. Legal
action is in all cases swift. The country is today among the most hospitable to foreigners, who are captivated by the easy politeness and
simple cordiality of the people. Under the spell of this patriarchal hospitality, I, for instance, found myself taken into a home near Houston,
the property of General Hunt, a Texian of impeccable character both
in his private and his public life.[6] For nearly a week, this weary traveler
enjoyed his hospitality, and every day new friends or strangers were
always showing up, all of whom were welcomed and honored alike by
the master of the house. I never saw a frown cloud his brow, unless
it be at the moment of leave-taking. One must go back through the
centuries to the Age of Gold to find models for this fraternal society,

---

younger than he; Crockett was his elder by seven years; Stephen F. Austin was
also born in 1793.

[6] Memucan Hunt (1807–1856) seems to have entertained all comers at this
period somewhat more generously than his future security would have dictated.
At the time when he was Gaillardet's host, Hunt was serving as Texan representative on the joint United States-Texas boundary commission. He continued
to be prominent in the affairs of the Republic and of the state, but "his last
years were spent in efforts to recoup his fortune" (C. T. Neu, "Hunt, Memucan," *The Handbook of Texas,* ed. Walter Prescott Webb, I, 864).

which so freely shares its bread and water; one must rise in one's imagination to the most polished and well-educated classes of our European cities to find examples of the urbanity one meets here in the wilderness.

One serious criticism that North Americans have continued to level against Texas is that it has no religion. This terrible accusation becomes practically an encomium, from the point of view of a foreigner like myself who has experienced and smarted beneath the intolerant meddling which so-called religious principles impose upon the public and private affairs of the Yankees. The Texians are religious, but there exists between them and their decriers that same difference in the matter which is observable between the North and West of the American Union: here, one sees believers; there, one meets only fanatics. I have heard all the warring sects of Protestant America tear into one another, never to be united except in their common denunciation of the Catholics. In Houston, I have witnessed a far more unusual sight, but also a much less distressing one. I have seen in one of the halls of the Capitol Building (no church has yet been erected) a Presbyterian minister delivering his sermon to his attentive followers; then, at the conclusion of his service, he escorted to the rostrum another minister, whom he introduced to the congregation in approximately these terms: "I welcome one of my colleagues, a gentleman of a different communion. He is of the Methodist faith. He is going to expound to you his ideas. Get all you can from this. He has brought along with him a roll book, in which any of you who will adopt his beliefs will be asked to write your names. I introduce him to you as a fine fellow, and I am confident that in any case you will be glad to have heard him."

The Methodist was then heard with rapt attention and with the result that three elderly women went forward to be inscribed as members of his church.

CHAPTER SIX

A Future for the French in Texas[1]

NEW YORK, JULY 24, 1839—Texas is on the whole a flat country. More prairie lands than wooded areas are to be found there. The prairies are magnificent, the most delightful sight an eye can hope to behold. For nine months of the year Texas is a green carpet decorated with wild flowers. It is a garden, where the hand of man has nothing to do but gather. Nature alone is sufficient to reproduce the treasures of this vast, fertile park in which every adornment and every fruit of the earth grow without cultivation. The Americans call Texas their Italy, their Andalusia. This praise is no exaggeration.

Although mountains are rare in Texas, hills abound. In most places, the terrain offers to the eye irregular and picturesque undulations, which extend like solid waves on a troubled sea. A reed sometimes grows in great profusion in the uneven furrows of this sea, reaching unbelievable heights and covering many miles. One such thicket rears its proud brow on the banks of Caney Creek; its slender, sinuous course

---

[1] This article was published in the *Journal des Débats,* October 26, 1839. Unlike the four preceding chapters, it was not reprinted in the *Courrier des États-Unis.*

extends for a distance of seventy miles!² A narrow path has been cut through this bamboo-like growth, and the traveler is sheltered by an impenetrable archway formed from the tall, lanky shoots interlaced and thickly matted overhead.

The forests which Texas possesses are usually located on river banks. More than in any other part of America one finds there those secular giants precious for ship building when their timber has been hardened by the elements. Forests of future masts rise up to the sky as they await the axe of the Americans, who have so far left them untouched. Only recently has the superiority of Texas wood been discovered. A special agent of the Russian embassy in Washington, D.C., was inspecting this untapped wealth at the time that I, in the company of Monsieur de Saligny, the commissioner from the French legation, was doing the same thing.

The products of Texas will, as time goes on, become infinitely more varied. The fertility of the soil, which, in all of North America, is perhaps unequaled except in the states of Indiana and Illinois; the mildness of the climate, Texas's heat being tempered by a steady cool breeze: these factors make it suitable for all types of agriculture, whether colonial or European. Even the grape, I am told, has been quite successfully cultivated. At present, the major crops of Texas are confined to cereals, sugar, tobacco, and cotton. The latter product furnishes the chief revenue of this budding economy. No sooner had Texian cotton made its appearance in foreign markets than its quality was recognized and acclaimed without contradiction. This cotton is of a golden-yellow hue and is unequaled by other varieties, both in strength and in length. It is always quoted at a higher price than all its rivals.

Texas covers an area of approximately five hundred square miles, including all regions to which it may properly lay claim; it occupies

² An 1839 map of Texas, in a series attributed to Stephen F. Austin, shows the stream flowing into the Gulf just east of Matagorda Bay. Inland on the map is marked the cane brake here described. Of the many creeks in Texas bearing this name, this is most probably the one described by Gaillardet (map reprinted in end papers of Eugène Maissin, *The French in Mexico and Texas* [*1838–1839*]).

today and has actually colonized four hundred square miles, or 25,-000,000 acres,[3] of which 5,000,000 to 6,000,000 are to be used exclusively for cotton. Assuming that these lands produce only one bale per acre, the minimum anticipated yield, the total production would be five million bales. Sold at $40.00 per bale, this would bring in $200,000,000 per year (a billion francs)! Twenty million acres would be left for other uses!

Thus we see the possible sources of future wealth for the country. I am now going to discuss the financial condition of the present government, as revealed by the secretary of the treasury in an official report, which M. de Saligny and I were permitted to consult. This document is an as yet uncompleted survey of the financial and military resources of the state, including its receipts and disbursements in the different branches of its organization. Before presenting an outline of it, I should explain that the financial system of Texas differs from that of the United States in that the government alone is the bank, issuing the paper, or treasury bonds, that constitutes the ordinary money of the country. The only Texas paper money in circulation is of national origin. It represents the debt of the state and not of any private enterprise whatsoever.

---

[3] Chester Newell, *History of the Revolution in Texas,* p. 129: "It embraces within its more generally known limits—on a line running from the 32d degree N. latitude, on the East, to the cross timbers on the West, *a distance of four hundred miles,* and from this line to the sea, *a distance of one hundred miles* —35,000 or 40,000 square miles, or 25,000,000 of acres . . ." (italics mine). Gaillardet, in borrowing from this passage, misunderstood the sentence structure and falsified the meaning. He took what Newell gave as boundary lines to be square mileage, obtaining the figure of five hundred square miles total area by adding together the length and breadth figures, four hundred and one hundred miles, respectively. The error is understandable from the pen of one accustomed to the metric system and not completely at home with the English language; moreover, Newell's complicated style in this sentence is likely to give even a native English speaker pause. Curiously, this error was perpetuated in Frédéric Leclerc's *Texas and Its Revolution,* p. 135: an indication of Leclerc's familiarity with Gaillardet's articles on Texas.

Summary of report furnished April 17, 1839, by Mr. James Webb, secretary of the treasury of Texas:[4]

Naval Force as Voted by Congress:
Eight seventy-gun ships, crew of 1,055 men each
One eighteen-gun ship, crew of 211 men
Two twelve-gun brigs, crew of 159 men each
Three seven-gun schooners, crew of 65 men each
One seven-gun steamship, crew of 105 men
One ten-gun steamship, crew of 132 men

Note: with the exception of the largest warships listed, Texas today possesses in its ports or in the Baltimore navy yards the totality of this naval strength.

Land forces:
In the case of a resumption of hostilities with Mexico, the government is authorized to recruit six regular regiments, of which one will be cavalry, one artillery, and four infantry. Twelve thousand trained militiamen can be gathered and made ready in less than thirty days.

In time of peace one regiment of fifteen companies, deployed between the Nueces and the Red Rivers, is sufficient defense against Indian depredations.

The expenses necessary for either of these alternatives will not exceed $350,000.

Imports and Exports:
From September 30, 1836, to September 30, 1838, imports amounted to $1,840,376; import duties brought a total, from the five land and sea customs houses of Texas, of $350,000.

However, the rapid increase in imports will be demonstrated by the only figures available to the government so far this year, those for the first quarter from the port of Galveston. The total in duties collected by customs in that city between September 30, 1836, and September 30, 1838, amounted to

---

[4] James Webb (1792–1856), a Virginian, had moved to Houston in 1838. A friend and adviser to M. B. Lamar, he served successively as secretary of the treasury, secretary of state, and attorney general of Texas (Hobart Huson, "Webb, James," *The Handbook of Texas*, ed. Walter Prescott Webb).

$163,637. The accounting for the first three months of this year [1839] shows that during this short space of time, one fourth of the year, the import duties came to $53,000, that is, nearly one third of what had been received during a previous period of two years! A similar rise is to be noted at the port of Matagorda, which up to the present has been the port with the heaviest traffic in Texas.

The survey of exports has not yet been completed, the only part available being that of exports to the United States. Cotton shipments to that country in the year 1838 amounted to $165,718.

National Debt:

Issuance of paper money, or promissory notes, since the establishment of the government	$1,098,453
Collections from import taxes and direct taxes since the law of the last session of congress	198,453
By virtue of this law, the sum collected cannot be circulated. There thus remain in circulation	$ 900,000
The total consolidated debt, retirable at the discretion of the government after 1842	667,800
The total of military debts and other obligations contracted with private individuals	248,000
Claims against the government, not yet liquidated estimated at	60,000
Total debt, strictly speaking	$1,875,800
To which might be added the expenses of civil branches of government for this year	400,000
Grand total of all that will be owed at the end of the present year, not counting, however, the expenses of the army and navy	$2,275,800

State Resources:

Customs duties, estimated for the present year on the basis of collections during the first months	$ 954,000
Payments on sale of land	564,000
Direct taxes	250,000
Sale of lots in city of Calhoun	500,000
Sale of lots in city of Austin, the future capital	500,000

Sale of lots in the city of Galveston 250,000

TOTAL $3,018,000

Total debt as of December 31, 1839 2,275,800

Balance in favor of the government . . . . $ 742,200

It must be considered, as well [says Mr. James Webb], that next year a million dollars will be collected for payment of land for which titles have already been delivered, or will be in the course of this year. It may likewise be assumed that direct taxes will reach a million dollars, judging by property rights being delivered during the current year for lands already sold, which will become subject to direct taxation, whereas hitherto they were untaxable so long as titles remained in the possession of the government.

Finally, the government possesses several million acres of land, the greater part of which is of unsurpassed quality. The progressive sale of this land is the sure source of an immense and unending flow of revenue.

Whoever will glance at a map of Texas and observe on it the numerous indications of *grants,* or private concessions, will wonder that there should remain at the disposal of the government such a large amount of land as the above-quoted document claims. It is therefore well to point out that the majority of the grants or concessions traced on the maps have been foreclosed and declared null and void. They emanated in large part from the Mexican government, which had been very liberal in this respect during the time of the first colonization efforts carried out in Texas. To each grant, however, were attached resolutory conditions such as, for instance, the condition of settling within a given time a certain number of colonists on the land which formed the area of the grant. None, or practically none, of the grantees fulfilled the stipulated terms by the time of the separation of Texas from Mexico. The new government declared the lapse of the legal time limit allowable to the delinquent *empresarios* and thus obtained an immense amount of national land. In spite of these legitimate foreclosures, the grantees of the original titles, their heirs and assigns did not scruple to place for sale on the markets of both sides of the Atlantic those titles which actually had been invalidated, although they appeared outwardly to be still legal. Hence arose the dreadful stockjobbing and fraudulent speculation on Texas land scrip, a counterfeit currency that brokers passed back and forth from America to Europe, from Europe to America.

Those underdeveloped lands of either real or imaginary ownership were sold then for fifteen or twenty cents an acre. Today, not an acre is to be had for less than one dollar, and many are worth ten dollars. This rise in the cost of land is owing to the fact that a year and a half ago Texas had only 40,000 inhabitants across its desert wastes; today the population is in excess of 250,000.

What have been the causes of this rapid increase? The richness of the soil, the location at the southern end of the American Union, and, one must add, the toleration by the new constitution of slavery without restrictions and without limit. The planters of Virginia, Georgia, and the two Carolinas have been beleaguered and pressed by the tireless abolitionist propaganda from the North. They possessed nothing except those originally poor lands that were quickly exhausted by the cultivation of tobacco. In throngs they are deserting such fields, which promise neither security nor fortune, and are moving lock, stock, and barrel to richer, more hospitable country. From the militant advance guard that they have been, they are passing to the rear guard.

In the enjoyment of this position lies the germ of Texas's future greatness. It will become, in the more or less distant future, the land of refuge for the American slaveholders; it will be the ally, the reserve force upon which they will rest and possibly fall back from Louisiana, Arkansas, Missouri, Kentucky, Tennessee, Mississippi, Florida, Alabama, Georgia, the two Carolinas, Virginia and all the slave states, whenever this issue of slavery, so pregnant with latent danger, shall at last erupt to sever the two opposing sides in America. If as a result of this schism or of any other incompatibility that great association, the American Union, should be one day torn apart, Texas unquestionably would be in the forefront of the new confederacy, which would be formed by the Southern states from the debris of the old Union.

For this reason the southern half of the United States strongly advocated annexation at the time when Texas, feeling so insecure as yet in its newly acquired independence, came knocking at the door of the American confederation. For the same reason the Northern states, on the contrary, voiced vigorous opposition to this expansion. For the first group Texas was an ally; for the others it was one more enemy. The majority of the Congress in Washington declared themselves in favor of a refusal, for motives of caution and political expediency which it is not without value to discuss at this point.

By annexing Texas, the American government would have been inviting a costly war with Mexico over an undeveloped country offering nothing to offset the costs of war. The territorial aggrandizement without any immediate increase in wealth or strength would have had the overwhelming disadvantage of arousing European suspicion and opposition and of forcing ambitious America to pause in its previously uninterrupted free expansion. The problems created for the future would have far outweighed the benefits of a present territorial gain. In the eyes of the most perspicacious Washington cabinet members, the annexation of Texas, premature by at least five or six years, would be tantamount to accepting an eighty per cent discount on that great claim bequeathed by destiny to the Anglo-Saxon race and embracing all of Mexico and the other Latin American countries.

By limiting its role to that of a simple protector of the interests of Texas and by giving the state the appearance of complete independence, the United States could make of it an adventurous outpost for more or less justified conquests, the responsibility for which would rest entirely outside the jurisdiction of the parent nation. Texas would become a valuable instrument for present-day expansion without risk of interruption and without prejudice to the future.

One cannot but admire the shrewdness of this plan, but it lies within the power of the European governments to upset it. They may do so by one simple policy. Shall I say what I have in mind? Recognition and maintenance of the *real* independence and nationality of Texas.

There is in the character of the Anglo-American race a marvelous facility for espousing, if I may so express it, the land upon which their wandering feet have come to rest, and for cutting off all ties with their former homeland. Once this break has been made, nothing remains in their hearts but the merest trace of an affectionate memory. American patriotism is local in nature; the national loyalty springs from individual prosperity. Wherever a man has a field, a family, or some hopes for making his fortune, there lies his true fatherland. This national tradition of civic ingratitude was first exemplified and passed on to the present generation when its inconstant forefathers rebelled against England, the cradle of their birth.

A further development of this defect or virtue, however you may choose to look at it, sprang from the resentment of the people of Texas against the Congress in Washington for the latter's refusal to accept their offer to join the Union. In vain the delegates of these shrewd, self-centered people sought to soften the blow by telling their constituents of the important part that Texas was called upon to play in the Anglo-American community. Texas saw but one fact at the heart of these great plans: it was to be used to pull somebody else's chestnuts out of the fire. It flatly rejected a role of such chivalrous self-sacrifice. Thenceforth, no longer were Americans to be found on the land extending from the Sabine to the Río Grande: people began to refer to themselves only as Texians. A nationalistic sentiment issuing from wounded pride grew with the help of continuing success. Now that it has firmly taken root in this soil, it would be difficult to eradicate. Texas has had too successful a start at being a nation to revert very willingly to the position of a mere state of the Union. The change which evolved in public opinion in Texas on this subject is now well known in the United States, and, if I am to judge by information drawn from certain highly reliable sources, the American government has more than once had occasion to view with regret the course that its own political circumspection has led Texas to adopt.

The best interests of the United States require that it exert, with all due secrecy, every effort to gradually bring Texas to a halt in this fatal course and back to the mother country. The best interests of European countries require that they exert as their official policy every effort to encourage Texian nationalism. For this reason they must recognize its independence. Without recognition the perilous financial state of the country will be prolonged, for its wealth, or paper representation thereof, will continue to be devalued;[5] the national independence will be jeopardized; ambitious America will perhaps get the chance to reimpose its control. With recognition, on the other hand, Europe insures the independence and prosperity of Texas. It restores to the national currency the value of which it was deprived by nothing other than speculation and uncertainty about the future.[6] To the south of the North American continent Europe secures a medium-sized state between the dreaded expansionism of the United States and the even more dreaded weakness of the Spanish-American states; Texas will obviously become much less dangerous to the latter than troublesome to the former. By this move, finally, Europe finds, among the Texian population themselves, a barrier against further Anglo-American extension southward; it is by Americans that it stops and contains the Americans.

Yet the benefits of such a policy will depend as much on speed of execution as on the execution itself. Texas desperately needs recognition by a major European nation, but it needs only one. It will perhaps pay dearly to obtain this baptism; once the first sacrament is acquired,

---

[5] "The currency of Texas loses up to 60 or 65 per cent of its face value on the money exchanges of the United States" (GN).

[6] A footnote repeating information from Gaillardet's letter of April 21, 1839, is inserted at this point, followed by a reminder of the signing of the Franco-Texian treaty of September 25; this note, presumably by the editor of the *Journals de Débats*, Bertin *l'Aîné*, was an effort to bring the article up to date, its publication being delayed by three months with respect to its date of composition: "The Texian government recently attempted to negotiate a loan of two million dollars. It was assured that the issuance of the loan would be immediate provided that, in addition to the guarantees already offered, it could add recognition by France and England of its independence. Hence the mission on which General Henderson was dispatched by the Texian government to these two countries.

"It will be recalled that a treaty of friendship, trade, and shipping was signed in Paris on September 25 between France and the Republic of Texas."

it will doubtless have no trouble getting the others without having to pay or beg.

France, in particular, has more at stake than any other nation in the solution of this question. Perhaps uniquely it has numerous special interests, which I shall discuss further on. Already we have concluded a treaty of commerce with the Texian envoy, but this is not enough. For England had done so before us; it had, before us, sent an agent to Texas to defend its interests there; before we can do so, it has already sent a ship, the *Ambassador,* the first to be sent directly from Europe to receive a cargo of Texas cotton; it will likewise be ahead of us and above us wherever it manages to slip up and equal us.

England would, I feel confident, long ago have recognized Texas were it not for its conflicting engagements with Mexico and its fear of losing its influence there as a result of having hurt the feelings of the Mexicans. Since we have no such interests, we have no such tact to maintain.

For three years Texas has in fact kept its independence, and no hostile act has occurred to threaten it. This is one of those well-established, irreversible situations we call *faits accomplis.* One hears loose talk of an imminent last attack that Mexico plots, after three years of avowed impotence. This attack will not take place, or if it does take place, it is not the future of Texas but of its enemy that will be jeopardized.[7]

It was thus a fortunate idea of the French government to send an agent to Texas to study and report back the truth about the country. Monsieur de Saligny, having been assigned to this important task, demonstrated all the more his efficiency and skill because his unofficial capacity demanded more than the usual caution and reserve. The man's

[7] "For a Mexican invasion to become a reality, it would have been necessary that the Federalist Party be extinguished by the death of Mejía. Instead, it has continued to flourish, vigorous and threatening, under the leadership of General Lemus, who has won a major victory at Saltillo. Therefore, a treaty of friendship is more likely than a war between Mexico and Texas. If war did come, Texas would at worst suffer losses of property and lives, but still the enemy would gain nothing and might have to pay very dearly" (GN).

extraordinary tact and perspicacity, which make him one of the most distinguished members of our legations, permitted him to scrutinize and evaluate not only those aspects of the country which the people were most eager to have him see, but especially whatever they least cared to publicize. Moreover, despite the restraint which he affected, despite his efforts to convince people that his visit was in the role of a private inquirer merely, the Texians received him with such cordiality that their friendship for France was clearly demonstrated. As I have previously pointed out, Texians are radically different from most North Americans in their social temperament. They are in large part emigrants from the Western regions and possess that vivacity of character and especially that combative spirit which is characteristic of the American frontiersman. France, its military prowess, and Napoleon are the great objects of their admiration and emulation: this is what they retain and love best out of all that they see or read of our Europe. President Mirabeau Lamar has, more than anyone else, this idolatry for a war-minded France. "Recognition by England would perhaps be no more difficult to obtain and no less useful to my country than French recognition," he said to Monsieur de Saligny in my presence, "but I personally as the chief executive of Texas and as a man of French descent should feel very much gratified if I could obtain recognition by France before any other."

These feelings were just as energetically expressed on the occasion of Admiral Baudin's tour of the country.

As I have stated, France has numerous special interests to consider in connection with the Texas question:

This burgeoning state might offer a valuable outlet to the products of our soil and factories. All that is consumed in Texas, from luxury items to the necessities of life, comes from New York or New Orleans and is sold at exorbitant prices. Those two sources are themselves to a large degree the warehouses of England, Germany, and France. In 1838 exports from the United States to Texas officially totaled $1,247,800.

By selling directly to Texas, France could expand its exports on all consumer goods, sharing its profits with no one and reducing the sales prices. The reduction in prices could be tremendous, especially if our government could obtain, for wine, for instance, a lowering of tariff barriers, which generally are no less than twenty to thirty per cent.

However, in the long run, the most valuable and far-reaching advantage that Texas could offer France would be as a place for emigration, a center for colonial expansion. Texas, of all parts of America, is the one which offers the immigrant the richest land, the easiest communications, and, above all, the greatest degree of protection on the part of the local authorities. By constitutional guarantee, every immigrant, upon becoming naturalized—that is, after six months of residence on Texas soil—has the right to a grant of three hundred acres of land. It is true that this unrivaled opportunity will expire in 1841.

If tomorrow the numerous groups who daily leave France in order to till the virgin soil of North America should agree to meet again in Texas; if, instead of scattering in the wilderness, where often they labor fruitlessly and are unrewarded for their pains, they should gather and join forces in this land of Texas, so rich in promise of gain, this French colony mingling with the American colony could render priceless service to the mother country. The original colonists would no doubt retain their supremacy over the newcomers by virtue of their prior settlement and greater numbers; but however slight might be the proportion of the Gallic family married to the Anglo-Saxon race, their presence would suffice to affect the political scene, their mentality would color the national character. When one considers, in addition to this interior influence, the strength which a French colony, however small it might be, would draw from its location in the immediate vicinity of Louisiana, the former French possession, where the spirit of our ancestors is still very much alive and more than ever at odds with the melting-pot philosophy of the new masters of the soil, is not a cursory glance sufficient to realize the consequences with which my subject of inquiry is pregnant?

The importance of this question had doubtless struck Monsieur

Mollien[8] before it struck me, when this most remarkable man among those whom France enjoys as its representatives abroad—Monsieur Mollien, the distinguished writer and seasoned world traveler, at present our consul general in Havana—wrote the following words. I can close my discussion in no better way than by quoting from memory a passage from a letter I received from him just before I traveled to Texas:

Go see this country and tell our France of the many resources it offers; go tell our emigrants especially. By converging there, they might multiply their strength, which is dissipated in isolation; they might create for themselves a refuge, where they would no longer be obliged to beg admittance, as ragged pilgrims rapping with their canes at a hostile gate. Remind them of the memories by which Texas is already linked to France, I mean that sad tale of Champ d'Asile;[9] show them finally what might be the future role of a Franco-Texian colony, placed like the beam of a balancing scale halfway between the two weights which share the Americas, the English and Spanish races; our own race—alas!—no longer possesses anything there!

[8] Gaspard-Théodore Mollien, born in 1796, was the son of François-Nicolas Mollien, Napoleon's finance minister from 1806 to 1815. As an explorer, Mollien *fils* discovered the sources of the Senegal and Gambia Rivers and journeyed extensively in the Republic of Colombia. He was the author of several volumes based on his travels. His later life was devoted to the consular service.

[9] Bertin here added the following footnote: "We shall soon publish our correspondent's report on the episode of the French at Champ d'Asile." This promise was never realized in the pages of the *Journal des Débats*. Instead, we find it two years later in the *Constitutionnel,* a rival Paris paper. It constitutes the tenth chapter of the present collection.

The Beginnings of Louisiana[1]

NEW YORK, DECEMBER 21, 1839—In the history of France, one period stands out as particularly brilliant and beautiful. I refer to the century of Louis XIV, when our country—illustrious in war, in science, and in industry—possessed uncontested hegemony in Europe and shared with Spain the forefront in the Americas. At that time, ours was truly a colossal people: with one foot firmly standing on one hemisphere, it reached its second across to the other. Louis XIV, burning with ambition for glory and triumph, could foresee great, incomparably great destinies for himself and his race. Among the dreams which lulled this monarch's brain, one of the most persistent and most deeply cherished was the hope of founding a New France on American shores. His pride swelled with the idea of this creation, which would have enabled him to say on his deathbed: "I was given

[1] This chapter and Chapters Eight and Nine appeared in the *Courrier des États-Unis* from the end of 1839 to the beginning of 1840 (the exact date of the New York publication is supplied at the head of each chapter). The first two of these had earlier appeared in the *Journal des Débats* (February 16 and August 4, 1839). The chief source of information for Chapter Seven is Charles Gayarré, *Essai historique sur la Louisiane*; the latter was, in turn, little more than a French version of François Xavier Martin's *History of Louisiana*.

one kingdom; I give back two. France will have from me as much again as I received from God!" France would have had indeed much more than that, for its overseas possessions were six times its own size. It possessed Canada and Louisiana, the Saint Lawrence and the Mississippi: the two arms and the two lungs of America, if we may think of that continent as a vast body whose brow rests on the Atlantic and whose feet stretch out into the immensity of the wilderness. Our flags formed a victorious rainbow, from the fort of the Balise[2] to New Orleans, from New Orleans to Fort Rosalie (today called Natchez), from Fort Rosalie to Fort Saint Louis, from Saint Louis to Fort Duquesne (today Pittsburgh), to Detroit, to Chicago, to Presqu'île (today Erie, Pennsylvania), to Michilimackinac, to Ticonderoga, to Vincennes, Indiana, to Fort Frontenac (today Kingston, Ontario), to the fort of Chartres, to Peoria, Montreal, Saint Johns on the Richelieu, Quebec, and Louisburg—a great curve from the Gulf of Mexico to the island of Cape Breton. What an empire! What a dream!

Today, one is filled with mingled bitterness and fascination as one studies the history of the discoveries, achievements, and events which first gave us, then took away, this great heritage. It is sweet to let the imagination dwell on this glorious past of our country, there to seek instruction for the present, and, if possible, hopes for the future—certainly no hopes like those which could and did shine forth in the age of Louis XIV; fate has irrevocably decreed against them. In classing nations according to its whims and in subjecting people to new social affinities, fate has not however broken the moral links which a common origin, identical language, and common heritage have forged. To seek to rekindle dying memories, to remind two oblivious peoples of their community of origin and language—the task seems valuable and worth while both for the homeland and for those who long were its honored children. That is what I realized while visiting our former possessions

---

[2] Balise, an island at the mouth of the Mississippi, was long the point at which pilots met ships heading upstream from the Gulf. Cf. Gustav Dresel, *Houston Journal: Adventures in North America and Texas, 1837–1841*, pp. 24, 42.

in America, especially in Louisiana, which was, with Canada, the largest of these possessions, the beloved land in which France planted one of its most luxuriant offshoots. That is what impelled me to write these pages and to offer them to you now.

In 1673 our Canadian posts seemed to be firmly and permanently established. The steep rock of Quebec was crowned with fortifications; Montreal was already founded; and Fort Richelieu, the fort of Lake Chambly, and another near Lake Champlain had been built. The savage tribes were submissive to the strength of our fighting men and to the Holy Gospel of our missionaries. They had recently recognized our authority in the course of a great powwow which they had held at Sault Sainte Marie. Our churchmen and our men of arms were joined in a common goal, that of opening up the unknown lands, the first in order to win souls for Christ, the rest to win new wealth for France. In the first category, Fathers Marquette and Hennepin were outstanding both for their fervor and for their genius as explorers. These sublime adventurers were accompanied by men including a certain Salignac de Fénelon, who dispensed among the savages of Lake Ontario the same heavenly manna, his polished oratory, which was shortly thereafter to be collected, drop by precious drop, in France by the most highly polished society in the world.[3] Every kind of labor, suffering, and devotion was undergone by these crusaders fighting for their faith, their only weapon being their faith itself, their only recognition or rewards being those which issued from their own hearts, their only witnesses being God and the wilderness. This is a celestial chapter in the book of our conquests, one which is too little known and too seldom vaunted. One of these missionaries was once led by simple charity to accompany some Indian families who were fleeing their homeland after it had been ravaged by the Iroquois. As he departed he

---

[3] There is a confusion here between, on the one hand, François de Salignac de Fénelon, Archbishop of Cambrai, the great writer and spiritual counselor of France's royalty, and, on the other, his elder half-brother who bore the same Christian name and who, after ordination in 1665 as a Sulpician priest, went to Canada as a missionary. Cf. Katherine Day Little, *François de Fénelon: Study of a Personality*, pp. 5, 18.

wrote to his superior: "I am with a party composed of sixty persons, including men, women, and children. All are in an extremely enfeebled condition. As for food, it is in the hands of Him who feeds the birds of the air. I set forth burdened with my sins and my wretchedness, and I have great need of your prayers on my behalf."

During an exploratory expedition toward the West, Father Marquette and a recent arrival in Canada, a certain Jolliet from Picardy,[4] both of whom had learned a smattering of the Indian tongues, heard the natives speak of the greatest blessing of the country, a faraway river that in their picturesque language they referred to as the Father of Waters (*Meschacebe*). On their return to their settlement, our two Frenchmen related to their companions the story, which was heard with much interest, for no one there had ever before heard of this stream. [Jean-Baptiste] Talon, the first intendant of New France, became convinced that this majestic river, whose course was completely unknown, would afford a passage to China by going upstream and an outlet upon the Gulf of Mexico by going downstream. Marquette and Jolliet, who shared his expectations, offered to devote themselves to this important discovery. They managed to get four Indians to act as guides, and with them they set out in simple birchbark canoes across Lake Michigan. By this means they safely reached Green Bay, and went up the Fox River, along which the tribe of the same name had their homes. Beyond this river they crossed a chain of steep mountains, which formed the divide between East and West, and beyond these mountains they followed another river, the Wisconsin. At last, on July 7, 1673, they were there: they had reached and discovered the Meschacebe, the gateway to so many lands, whose melodious name was later altered to Mississippi to correspond more closely to the Iroquois word. Henceforth, America would have an outlet to the South, just as it already had one to the North! . . . As a ritual, the four Indians cast arrows, calumets, flowers,

---

[4] Louis Jolliet (1645–1700) was actually a native of Quebec, who embarked upon a career of exploration only after studies in Europe which equipped him as an expert cartographer. Cf. Louise Phelps Kellogg, "Jolliet, Louis," in *Dictionary of American Biography*.

and ears of corn into the Nile of their savage land; all hailed the Father of Waters, which the natives considered as merely a river, while the others glimpsed an empire. It is related that good Father Marquette, in a naïve ecstasy of delight, entoned a *Te Deum,* dipped his hands into the Meschacebe and blessed with the water of the new Jordan all the objects around him. Meanwhile, Jolliet was kicking up dirt with his foot and uttering cries of victory at finding it to be very fertile land.

Soon both were on their way again, allowing the mighty torrent to carry them along and to reveal the mouths of the Missouri, Ohio, and Arkansas, the three principal tributaries, in turn. Then they stopped, for their supplies were running low, turned about, and went northward, suffering incredible exhaustion. They reached another tributary, the Illinois, and followed its banks as far as the heights which separate the river from Lake Michigan. Here our two explorers parted, after long sharing their untold courage and patience in common. Father Marquette went humbly and simply to resume his evangelical work among the Miami Indians; Jolliet, on the contrary, sailed to Quebec to report to Governor Frontenac the results of their partnership in exploration. The cathedral bells tolled throughout the day of his arrival, and the bishop, accompanied by other clergymen and the entire French population, entered to offer thanks to the Almighty.

The sensation produced by this great event, however, gradually subsided. Marquette, the saintly old man, died.[5] Jolliet was absorbed in his business affairs. Their discovery remained unexploited until one resolute man took it upon himself to continue the work. The man was a native of Rouen named Robert Cavelier de La Salle. He had for long been a member of the Society of Jesus, but on the death of his parents he had given up the priesthood. Being denied an inheritance from his parents' estate by virtue of his civil death, which his entry into a religious order had entailed, La Salle went to Canada to seek his fortune. There he engaged in both agricultural and commercial pursuits. Active, ambitious, possessed of a mind to conceive bold designs and of a firmness of will power to carry them out, La Salle urged Governor Frontenac to

[5] Marquette lived only thirty-eight years (1637–1675).

allow him to finish the task that Marquette and Jolliet had begun. He proposed to explore the Mississippi to its mouth if the necessary supplies were put at his disposal. Frontenac advised him to submit his plans personally to the court of France. La Salle accordingly set sail at once. The Prince de Conti and [Jean-Baptiste] Colbert became interested, and communicated their interest to Louis XIV. A ship, some men, and provisions were entrusted to La Salle. A worthy officer, [Henry] Squire de Tonti, joined the expedition.[6] La Salle and he left La Rochelle on June 14, 1678, after receiving from the king two sealed parchments, one of which granted La Salle command of Fort Frontenac, the other an exclusive right for fur trading in whatever regions he might discover.

Reaching Quebec on September 15, 1678, he conducted his party as far as Lake Ontario, where he directed repairs on Fort Frontenac before proceeding farther. Next, losing no time, he constructed a ship, crossed Lake Ontario, built a new fort at the opposite end of it, visited the neighboring country, and established relations with several tribes, while awaiting the hasty construction of a second ship on Lake Erie. In August, 1679, he set sail with forty men, among whom was Father Hennepin, the worthy successor of Marquette. They crossed the strait which separated them from Lake Huron, crossed that lake, reached Lake Michigan, then the Saint Joseph River, on which they erected a fort. There they were joined by Tonti, who had followed a different route. Together they all went up the Saint Joseph and entered the Illinois, which their predecessors had mapped. On its bank they built the fort of Crèvecœur, then they reached the Mississippi, as Marquette and Jolliet had before them.

The latter had chosen first to go downstream; La Salle decided first to go upstream. The others had directed their steps and their dreams toward the Gulf of Mexico; the present group directed theirs toward

---

[6] "He was an Italian officer, the son of the well-known inventor of the tontine. He had served with distinction in Sicily where he had lost a hand. Instead, he used a copper hand with extraordinary dexterity" (GN). Cf. Gayarré, *Essai historique,* I, 32–33.

long-sought China; before discovering the mouth of the Mississippi, they wished to find the easiest access to Canada, so as to join the colony to the river, the present America to its future.

On February 28, 1680, then, Father Hennepin went up the Mississippi in a bark canoe with two other Frenchmen and explored its numerous tributaries, both on the east and on the west. Going up the River Saint Pierre, they suddenly caught sight of a seventeen-foot falls that the river made ahead of them. To this cataract our travelers gave the name Sault Saint Anthony, after the patron saint of the day of the discovery; they drew their canoe ashore, carried it overland to the next stream, upon which they re-embarked, after baptising it with the name of Saint Francis. At last, they came upon a tribe of Indians, called the Sioux. Our men calmly approached them; the Sioux seized them and held them prisoner. The prisoners were soon on good terms with their new masters, however; three of the principal chieftains, who had lost their own children, adopted them as their sons and took them along on all their hunts and other expeditions. After three months of this life they obtained their release. Accepting the Indians' permission that they should depart, they went down the Mississippi to the Wisconsin, upstream on it to Michilimackinac, thence back to Montreal.

In the meantime, La Salle had remained with the Illinois Indians, whom he did not want to leave until he had established trading posts among them. His work was hindered by the plots of secret agents, both Indian and European, and by the rivalry of some Frenchmen as well, his disloyal companions. La Salle's life was once endangered by a poison that a fratricidal hand slipped into his food on Christmas day. It is said that he neutralized the effects of the poison with a theriac antidote and, once the danger was past, continued to carry out his plans all the more determinedly. When war broke out between the Illinois, his hosts, and the Iroquois, their enemies, he thought it necessary to protect his new establishments from any acts of hostility; for this purpose he erected on a cliff two hundred feet high, overlooking the river, Fort Saint Louis, the nucleus of a great city to be. Forced to leave part

FRÉDÉRIC GAILLARDET.

Plate 2. Frédéric Gaillardet as a young man, from an anonymous portrait first printed in the *Almanach administratif, historique et statistique de l'Yonne, année 1883*. Courtesy Bibliothèque Nationale, Paris.

LE GÉNÉRAL CHARLES LALLEMAND,

(BARON,)

Grand Croix de l'Ordre de Danebroc

Comandeur de l'Ordre Royal de la Légion d'Honneur.

Né le 25 Juin 1774 à Metz Dép.t de la Moselle.

(Les Lauriers seuls y croissent sans culture)

Champ d'Asile.

Plate 3. General Charles Lallemand, an engraving from a portrait by François-Henri Mulard (1769–1850). In the lower right corner is printed a line from a song about Champ d'Asile. Courtesy the Cabinet des Estampes, Bibliothèque Nationale, Paris.

Plate 4. Pierre Soulé at the age of fifty-eight (c. 1860), from an engraving by Jules Chauvet showing also a scene in New Orleans at which Soulé is using his eloquence to contain an angry mod. Courtesy the Cabinet des Estampes, Bibliothèque Nationale, Paris.

Draw by J.Champagne.

MLLE GEORGES

Plate 5. Mademoiselle Georges, a lithograph by J. Champagne dated 1856, but representing her as much more youthful than she could have appeared in her late sixties. Courtesy the Cabinet des Estampes, Bibliothèque Nationale, Paris.

of his men to defend the fort, he returned to Canada to enlist new troops; then, on February 2, 1682, he reached the banks of the Mississippi once more. This time he determined to go all the way down this giant river whose length was unknown and incalculable. When he had already traveled two hundred leagues downstream, he had merely reached the Arkansas, where Jolliet and Marquette had previously stopped; he went on. A hundred leagues more were covered, and still the river did not end; his companions eyed one another with disturbed glances. Still he kept on, however, and after a total journey of four hundred leagues he reached the Mississippi delta, which his companions had despaired of ever seeing. He performed a solemn ceremony of claiming it as a possession of France and gave these boundless lands the name of Louisiana, which they would ever after retain even though they were to be circumscribed.

Then, as now, the Mississippi was a murky torrent, rolling its yellowish waters along a channel that often measured eight hundred to a thousand yards in width, and emptying into the Gulf of Mexico by seven mouths fanning out in several directions. These seven outlets were originally just one. They developed by the accumulation of matter constantly being coughed up by the river water and forming a tumorous growth which strangled ever more tightly the river's course and impeded the flow with its numerous polyps. The lower banks were enormous swamps covered with scum and reeds; the upper banks, scarcely higher in elevation, offered for three hundred leagues a monotonous shore of forests, constantly subject to inundation from the river. The doomed trees, engulfed by the water, their great branches cast down and their foliage bespattered, gradually sank into the mire and became the scraggy skeletons and stumps which form hazards at the water's edge and even in its center. On the Red River, one of its tributaries, this forest debris was amassed and combined in such a way that it formed a bridge or floating raft across the whole river. A loam accumulated on top of this platform, from which new trees grew up, and thus an arm of the forest was suspended above the water. This strange flying buttress was finally destroyed by the hand of man or of time.[7]

Among the fruits which the soil of Louisiana produced, according to the early narratives, were olives, dates, and bananas. No trees for these fruits are to be found there today. Were it not for the respect which we owe to the word of our fathers, we should be tempted to state that such trees were never grown there. At least we may say that Mother Nature would be a most harsh stepmother for them today, since she could not even save and nourish the simple orange trees which have been planted on her humid breast. One notes likewise the disappearance of the ocelot, the cougar, the beaver, and the buffalo, all of which animals of the Canadian lake country have been said, doubtless through error, to inhabit Louisiana. On the other hand, the mosquito, the gnat, rats more numerous than men, the rattlesnake, the crocodile, these pests of the earth, air, and water, remain as more faithful guests of these parts. The last two mentioned are, one must add, remarkably unaggressive.

One of the chief products of the prairies appears to have been the wild oats, which gave their name to a native tribe. To fertilize the prairie, the Indians had recourse to fire. The ashes of the weeds increased the fertility of the soil, and from beneath this natural fertilizer sprang valuable new grass to feed the herds. To limit the extent of the fire, opposite ends of a field were set ablaze. Fire thus faced fire. The two lines were drawn together by mutual attraction, and the area between grew gradually smaller until the flames became concentrated in a single spot and died out. This method, based upon a very simple physical law, is still practiced in our own day.

We have perhaps wandered too far from our real subject—La Salle at his most active and fortunate stage. Already he has returned to Quebec and from there has set sail for France. He will carry home the keys to Louisiana, having done just what he had promised: to open this land to French domination. He prays that the homeland will take ad-

---

[7] According to Frédéric Leclerc, this gigantic impediment to navigation was destroyed by man, by order of the state legislature of Louisiana (Leclerc, *Texas and Its Revolution*, p. 23).

vantage of what is offered. Four vessels and 280 persons, including soldiers, farmers, laborers, and a few women are entrusted to La Salle to form a first colony. He departs with joyful heart and high hopes for the future—deceptively good auspices!

When they reached the Gulf of Mexico, December 28, 1684, Beaujeu, the fleet commander, mistook his bearings. After seeking in vain the Mississippi, the sure hope and haven of La Salle, he lent a deaf ear to the latter's counsels and entreaties and set him ashore, with his band of settlers, at the entry to Saint Bernard Bay, far west of the Mississippi. Beaujeu allowed the colony to keep only one ship on this unknown shore; he returned to France with the three others.

Indians soon appeared. La Salle was encouraged when he recognized weapons and canoes of a design similar to those he had observed among the natives of the Mississippi. He concluded that he could not be far from that long-sought stream. The Indians, however, appeared distrustful and fierce, and gave him no information. He was about resolved to exploring the coastline, when a storm broke out. His ship, his only ship, was wrecked on the shore. May the will of God be done! La Salle built two forts, one at the entrance to the bay, the other two leagues inland, near the Lavaca River, on a rise overlooking a plain. Hereafter, hunting and fishing would have to suffice for all their needs. Very soon, however, disease took its frightful toll. La Salle abandoned the first fort and concentrated his entire colony within the second.

Meanwhile, carrying out the agreement he had made with La Salle, the trusted Tonti was on his way southward from the Illinois territory, heading down the Mississippi to make contact with his friend. He spent several months in fruitless waiting; to no avail he sent out two canoes along the Gulf shore to search the coast. This quest was as fruitless as his wait had been. He went upstream to Crèvecœur, whence he had come. Along the way, several men yielded to the lure of adventure and left the party to live among the Cenis and Arkansas Indians. Temporarily lost to civilization, they were to become the nucleus of later, more thorough European penetration.

La Salle's position grew progressively worse. The passive unfriendliness of the Indians shifted to aggressive hostility. The crops of the colony were ravaged by the savages and wild animals, who were in league against the white men. Hunger was present, and revolt, its offspring, was not far behind. La Salle, whose courage outstripped his luck, and who vainly sought to break through the hopeless barrier of infinity and wilderness around him, resolved to go to the ocean's edge and reutter his cry for help and pity, to which the land had not responded with a single echo. For six months he followed the shore and recorded successively the discovery of the streams he named the Caney, the Colorado, the Sablonnière, and the Maligne[8]—all of them deserted, alas, and barren of hope for his rescue. A second expedition was later undertaken; in each he lost half of his followers. Early in the year 1687 there remained only thirty-seven men. He set out with sixteen of them on a new expedition to the Cenis country, undaunted, unshaken, determined to discover the way to Canada or perish in the attempt. In the band were two brothers named Lancelot.[9] The younger was of a weak constitution and, after two days of travel, was unable to keep pace with the others. He was forced to return to the fort; his brother asked permission to accompany him. This request was refused, for La Salle did

---

[8] Gaillardet's original is so punctuated as to indicate that the Sablonnière and the Colorado are two separate streams. Modern studies identify them as one and the same, by its French and Spanish appellations. The French word *Sablonnière* is the family name of one of La Salle's fellow explorers. The Maligne is identified as the Spanish *Brazos de Dios*. Cf. Émile Lauvrière, *Histoire de la Louisiane française, 1673–1939*, p. 53.

[9] Lancelot, the name that Gaillardet assigns to one of La Salle's murderers, the death of whose brother was the principal cause of the tragedy, is variously spelt in other histories as Liotot, Lanctot, Lanquetôt, and Lancelot. The early chroniclers of the assassination agree that the loss of the younger brother of this man occurred during a different, earlier journey out from the fort near Matagorda Bay (cf. Henry E. Chambers, *A History of Louisiana: Wilderness, Colony, Province, Territory, State, People*, I, 39–42; Régine Hubert-Robert, *L'Histoire merveilleuse de la Louisiane française: Chronique des XVIIᵉ et XVIIIᵉ siècles et de la cession aux États-Unis*, pp. 42–45. Gaillardet follows Gayarré in the spelling *Lancelot,* as well as in the grouping of the deaths of the younger Lancelot, of La Salle's nephew, and of La Salle himself, all on the same fatal trek (cf. Gayarré, *Essai historique,* I, 57–59).

not wish to lose anyone else from his already small party. The young man therefore went off alone and was assassinated by Indians. This news reached the camp of the explorers, and the elder Lancelot swore to avenge the death of his brother, for which he blamed La Salle.

After they had been two months on the move, their food supply became exhausted, and it was necessary to hunt for game. This caused them to separate into small groups. The salutary bond of discipline was necessarily slackened by this dispersion. One day, La Salle ordered Lancelot and a few others to go hunting under the leadership of his nephew. The latter felt compelled to punish some acts of insubordination among his hunters. Lancelot seized upon the resulting ill feeling as an opportunity to plan his revenge with the support of the insubordinate ones. They bided their time until a halt was called for rest, and then murdered the young officer in his sleep, along with two other men in his service. Once this crime was perpetrated, Lancelot easily convinced the murderers that their eventual capture and punishment could only be avoided by a second crime. La Salle became worried about the delay in the return of his nephew and went out in search of him on the third day of his absence. He caught sight of Lancelot in the distance and called out: "Where is my nephew?"

"There!" replied the fierce soldier, pointing with his finger to a mound of freshly turned dirt. At the same instant, one of his accomplices, who lay hidden in some tall grass, fired upon La Salle; the shot pierced his skull. La Salle survived his wound for only an hour. A missionary and a redskin, who were with him, witnessed him draw his last breath, March 19, 1687, near the western fork of the Trinity River.

Thus La Salle—of that inflexible arm, clairvoyant mind, and heroic courage, to whom France and Louisiana are eternally indebted—died in the midst of the wilderness, but ironically by the hand of a French assassin. To the sorrow which the indignity of his death stirs in our hearts, we must add another: according to Michel Chevalier,[10] nothing

[10] Michel Chevalier (1806–1869), the French economist early associated with Saint-Simon's socialistic movement, published *Lettres sur l'Amérique du Nord* in 1836. A third, revised edition appeared in 1838. Generally favorable toward

in all the vast American Union today recalls this noble name to the eye and mind, with the one exception of a small bust in the rotunda of the Capitol in Washington, somewhat lost between those of Penn and Captain John Smith, a legislative act of charity offered by the Congress to a neglected hero. Why so little?

La Salle's death carried off all hope of establishing at that time a permanent colony in Louisiana. His grief-stricken friends desired to avenge his murder, but a missionary, the *abbé* Cavelier—his brother— restrained them and pleaded that they should leave the task of vengeance to God. The task was soon accomplished. Two of the conspirators were killed in a quarrel among themselves, and the others disappeared voluntarily into the wilderness, not desiring to associate any longer with the explorers by whom they were regarded with unmixed horror.

Reduced to seven persons, the group continued their travels among the tribes of the Cenis, the Natchitoches, and others, all of whom received them hospitably and offered them the calumet of peace. Four months after the murder of La Salle they reached the mouth of the Arkansas. There a surprise awaited them: they beheld from afar a cross and a European dwelling! Upon running madly towards this sight, they found two Frenchmen of Tonti's expedition who, as previously

American society and government, Chevalier reported however a certain prevalent Yankee coldness of character, religious bigotry, narrowness of views, and austere self-denial. In contrast, the Western frontiersman impressed him as more hospitable, easygoing, and expansive. Gaillardet obviously borrows from Chevalier when he makes remarks in a similar vein (pp. 59–60, 61, 73); he had had no personal experience with Northern society when he wrote these pages. The repeated comparison of Texans to the ancient Romans (pp. 57,60) also had its source in Chevalier's work. The greatest debt which Gaillardet's study of American character owes to Chevalier is in the pages which contrast the energy of the Anglo-American colonists with their Spanish counterparts' idle ways (pp. 16–19); Chevalier's similar development of the subject concludes, as Gaillardet does, with the prediction of Anglo-American domination of the continent. Cf. Chevalier, *Lettres sur l'Amérique du Nord: Extraits*, pp. 12–21 (on the different American types); p. 49 (on the analogy with the ancient Romans); and pp. 41–43 (on the differences between English and Spanish colonizers).

related, had stopped there. Having been refreshed and oriented by these unexpected brethren, they went up the Mississippi and the Illinois to Fort Saint Louis, where they spent the winter, and thence to the Great Lakes. They finally reached Quebec on October 9.

As for the stranded ones whom La Salle had left at the fort of Saint Bernard Bay, the savages lost no time in attacking them. All were massacred, with the exception of five children, whose tender age was responsible for their being spared. These eventually fell into the hands of the Spanish and were aboard a Castillian ship nine years later when it was captured by the Chevalier Désaugiers. It was thanks to this encounter that the facts above related became known.

CHAPTER EIGHT

Iberville, Bienville, and Périer[1]

NEW YORK, DECEMBER 24, 1839—After La Salle's murder and the disappearance of the colony that he had founded to the north of Saint Bernard Bay, several years elapsed without further French attention to Louisiana. War confined all our strength and activity to Europe. The colonies started in Arkansas, Missouri, and Illinois were thrown entirely upon their own resources. Agriculture was tedious and land clearing was difficult, so hunting and fur trading became the chief means of subsistence and the only occupations of our colonists. Driven by necessity and by mutual rivalry, they formed that fearless group of

---

[1] A comparison of this chapter with Charles Gayarré's treatments of the same subjects reveals some startling parallels. The events and anecdotes related by Gaillardet are all to be found in Gayarré. In the earlier French version, the *Essai historique sur la Louisiane* (I, 60–116), the sequence of the narrative as well as the choice of words coincide so closely as to leave no doubt of Gaillardet's indebtedness. Even in Gayarré's later, more detailed account in English (*History of Louisiana: The French Domination*), the same material is covered in somewhat different sequence: the principal page references in the latter, listed in the order which corresponds to Gaillardet's treatment, are: 30–39; 57–70; 242; 234–235; 287; 143–150; 396–452.

poachers known as the *coureurs de bois.*[2] Their immoderate plundering soon produced the twin consequences of exterminating the game and alienating the Indians, who saw in this disastrous competition the loss of their only source of trade with the white men. Hence arose enmities which were later to explode in bitterest warfare.

The Peace of Ryswick (September, 1697) at last allowed France, after a ten-year lapse, to direct an eye toward its neglected children in the wilds of Louisiana. A fine seaman volunteered to go out to consolidate the chain of discoveries begun by La Salle in these regions. This seaman, of the stamp of the Jean Bart and Duguay-Trouin,[3] was named Iberville. With his brothers, he had distinguished himself during recent naval campaigns. Among his bold adventures, the following is most remarkable: being separated by a storm from the squadron to which he belonged, Iberville was assaulted by three enemy vessels which ordered his surrender, not expecting him to resist their superior strength. By way of reply, he sank the first ship, captured the second, and pursued the third, which escaped him only by the merest chance.

Two ships were placed under this courageous man's command. He set sail from Rochefort on October 17, 1698, anchored at the Cape of Santo Domingo, departed once more on the following New Year's Day, and headed for Pensacola Bay, where the Spanish had a short time earlier founded a small colony. Iberville explored Mobile Bay (today the location of a thriving city), Dauphin Island, the Pascagoula River, and Biloxi Bay; he reached the mouth of the Mississippi on March 2, 1699. He sailed upstream, still uncertain as to whether he was actually in the region which had been the theater of La Salle's explorations. His perplexity on this score was dispelled by a happy circumstance: a letter sent thirteen years before by Tonti to "La Salle, the Governor of Louisiana," had fallen into the hands of an Indian chief; Iberville was

---

[2] We leave in French the phrase *coureurs de bois* (literally, *wood runners*), as there appears to be no handy English equivalent.

[3] Jean Bart (1650–1702) and René Duguay-Trouin (1673–1736) were famous privateers whose names live on in legend and the French imagination, much as those of their contemporaries Captain Kidd and Sir Henry Morgan do among English-speaking peoples.

shown this precious document, which reviewed the events of his predecessors' various expeditions and described the signs which they had erected to indicate the terminal point of each trip.

Thus oriented, Iberville continued up the Mississippi as far as an outlet which his crew named for him. From it he discovered Lakes Maurepas and Pontchartrain and returned to Biloxi Bay, which he considered suitable to become the center of French colonization in Louisiana. There he constructed a fort, which he later abandoned because of its unstrategic location. Another was built at Mobile, but it too was given up in favor of one on Dauphin Island. Storehouses and barracks were built in 1702 on this island, which remained for some time the headquarters of the establishment.

Iberville failed to realize that the heart of the colony should be located on the vital artery running through the region; he was not, however, unaware of the tremendous importance of the Mississippi. He erected the fort of Balise at the entrance to the river. After much activity of this sort, he returned to France to awaken interest and support for the colony he had founded and was directing. During his absence his two brothers, Sauvolle and Bienville, valiantly assumed the leadership. Sauvolle, who was older, was in charge of the interior affairs of the colony; Bienville, the younger, took over the affairs of defense and sought to establish contacts with the Indian tribes.[4]

He was going home after one of these expeditions when he beheld a sixteen-gun British warship ahead of him at anchor on the Missis-

---

[4] According to Alcée Fortier (*A History of Louisiana,* I, 33), Charles Le Moyne had fourteen children, including the three brothers mentioned by Gaillardet: Pierre, sieur d'Iberville (1661–1706); Jean-Baptiste, sieur de Bienville (1680–1768); and François-Marie, sieur de Sauvolle, killed by Indians in 1687. Sauvolle's dates are elsewhere given as 1670–1700 (article "Le Moyne" in *Encyclopedia Canadiana*). The person whom Iberville left in charge of things in 1699 was possibly a different Sauvolle. Aware of the confusion, Dunbar Rowland states that "the first governor after Iberville of the French empire of the far west succumbed [to yellow fever], dying on August 22, 1701. If not a brother of the brilliant Le Moynes, he had won that place in the hearts of both brothers with whom he had combined his strength and talents in founding the colony" (*History of Mississippi: The Heart of the South,* I, 176).

sippi.[5] A strip of land forming a bend in the river had forced the British ship to stop and wait for a favorable wind before it could navigate the curve. When questioned by Bienville, the captain informed him that he had a second vessel of equal strength at the mouth of the river and that he came by governmental order to explore the Mississippi and to determine the advisability of establishing colonies on its banks. He asked Bienville whether the river on which they met were not indeed the one he had orders to explore. Bienville hastened to assure him that the Mississippi was much farther westward and that the river on which they were then anchored was a dependency of the French Canadian colonies. The credulous captain accepted this information gratefully and withdrew. The site of this successful stratagem then received the name of the English Turn, which it has retained to this day.

Iberville returned from France in December, 1699. Shortly thereafter, he received the unexpected visit of the Chevalier de Tonti, La Salle's trusted friend and fellow explorer. He had stayed with the Illinois Indians until he had heard news of a French colony in Louisiana. Then, with a company of seven men, he had immediately set forth down the Mississippi to investigate the report. The three brothers received with open arms this new brother in courage and sublime steadfastness. Iberville and Bienville went back with him as far as the plateau occupied by the Natchez tribe; there Bienville determined to locate Fort Rosalie,[6] which the evil genius of these regions foreordained to become the arena of a bloody combat in future days. Then they parted company after pledging to join hands ever after from their respective retreats and to form a holy triangle of friendship across Louisiana. This pact should have assured the future success of the colony.

Now, though, the fortunes of Louisiana were to suffer a reversal of

[5] The anecdote of Bienville's deception as related in French by Gayarré (*Essai historique,* I, 69–70) contains much of the same wording as Gaillardet's French—conclusive proof of Gaillardet's use of the earlier history. However, Gaillardet exhibits here a characteristic regard for concision: he reduces to 166 words a paragraph containing 219 words in Gayarré.

[6] "This was the Christian name of the Countess of Pontchartrain" (GN).

European origin. France was again plunged into a hazardous war that caused much blood to flow. When at last Marshal de Villars broke through the defenses of Denain and seized in his soldierly grip a victory and a peace, twin deities that had eluded the trembling fingers of an aging Louis XIV, then the all-consuming preoccupation of the Court of France was to nurse the public wounds. A speculator, [Antoine] Crozat, came forth to propose that he be granted the right to colonize and develop Louisiana. The offer was accepted, and an exclusive commercial charter was granted him in 1712 by the government, which retained nothing but the sovereignty and central administration of the country. Crozat bankrupted Louisiana and himself; in 1717 he relinquished the charter.

A company called the Occidental was bold enough to solicit and obtain the right to succeed him; a new charter was issued by the government for a twenty-five-year lease and far more extensive rights: a commercial monopoly; land, port, and island grants, except for nominal French sovereignty; a private naval force; exemption from payment of import duties; the right to declare war or conclude a peace; control of troop movements; judicial authority; and mineral rights. Mining! That was the magic word, the labarum of the affair, which was to allure and ensnare both large and small investors! On the strength of the existence of a copper deposit discovered long ago by the explorer Nicolas Perrot in the valley of the Saint Pierre River, the directors of the Compagnie d'Occident endowed the soil of Louisiana with every imaginable treasure. From the copper mines sprang silver mines, and then came the gold mines; diamonds and pearls poured unceasingly down the Mississippi. The head of the Compagnie d'Occident, the man behind the scenes who had organized the enterprise as it then existed and had in all probability invented its future marvels as well, was (and this explains everything) the infamous [John] Law. Having failed to find a European base for his banking schemes, he had been forced as a last resort to locate them on the nebulous reaches of the Mississippi.

To form the capital of the company, shares were issued at five hundred pounds each, the value of which was payable to the bearer in government paper money. These shares rapidly rose to over 100,000,-000, with the wealth of Louisiana as security. The wild orgy of speculation which ensued did not fail to benefit the development of the colony. Holders of important grants migrated to it, taking laborers with them; numerous communities were formed.

The company had contracted to transport to Louisiana six thousand whites and three thousand Negroes during the period of its charter. Eight hundred persons were sent in 1718. Dauphin Island had been ravaged by English pirates in 1710; the entrance to the port had been obstructed with sand during a hurricane in 1717. The headquarters and warehouses of the colony were therefore transferred once again to Biloxi Bay. Iberville's reasons for abandoning the station had, however, been all too sound, as tragic events were soon to demonstrate. The wretched colonists, cast upon a barren shore, were without means of livelihood or escape. Many perished, while the rest were saved only by the kind offices of the Indians, with whose help they dispersed to the settlements of Pascagoula, Baton Rouge, and Natchez, and to the Red, Arkansas, Ohio, and Illinois Rivers.

The day had come for New Orleans. The Mississippi, that king of rivers, was waiting to receive the queen of cities. A solid foundation for construction required that the location be forty leagues inland. Toward the coast, between the Mississippi and the sea, the soil forms a tongue which was, and still is, nothing but a mass of wood and mud accumulated probably as a result of the battle between the ocean and the river, as they invade and repel each other by turns. In the unceasing struggle of these two gigantic powers, the river has won this marshy jetty stretching forty leagues and ever farther into the realm of its enemy; the latter, for its part, has piled up dikes at the mouths of the river, treacherous bars to threaten it with suffocation.[7]

---

[7] "The force and volume of the Mississippi are such that its muddy river water covers that of the Gulf of Mexico for a distance of ten leagues. There the demarcation is clear and abrupt, as if a line had been drawn with a giant ruler. The passes of the Mississippi today have a depth of only thirteen or four-

The plan of New Orleans, said to be patterned after that of Roche-fort, was drawn up by Bienville, who had become governor of Louisi-ana after the death of his two brothers, Sauvolle and Iberville. The first had been the victim of disease and a mental breakdown, the second of an attack of yellow fever in Santo Domingo. One of the streets of New Orleans perpetuates the name of its founder. The first inhabitants arrived in the year 1718. It was not long before the Spanish, at odds with the French, attempted to seize it. The young city was, however, able to keep its virgin purity unsullied. The headquarters of the colony were transferred to it, and Bienville took up residence there. Louisiana enjoyed a moment of prosperity: colonists arrived in larger numbers, two additional forts were built, one on the Tombigbee River, the other on the Alabama. Together with Fort Rosalie, already built on the plateau of the Natchez, they comprised a system of defense the wisdom of which was abundantly demonstrated in the all too immediate future.

For many years the Indians among whom the Europeans had come and settled had reacted with mere placid curiosity toward these men who came from another world and appropriated parts of their lands and forests. As there was enough to go around, the Indians had no reason to object to the intrusion. The good natives gladly welcomed and gave assistance to men who, they considered, must have lacked in their own country sufficient food, or enough wood and fur to protect them-selves from the cold, for they had crossed perilous seas in search of these commodities. The Indians' peaceful acceptance gave way to sus-picion and alarm as successive waves of new arrivals pushed them ever farther to the hinterland, absorbed their resources, and surrounded them with forbidding fortifications. The Chickasaw and Natchez na-tions, whose territories were closest to the new colonies, were the most numerous. The former of these tribes was the first to become alarmed and hostile, while the latter continued much longer to be friendly and co-operative.

The Natchez were the most civilized of all Indian peoples. They had

---

teen feet at high tide. No ships displacing a greater depth of water can enter except by means of steamboats which tug them over the bottom" (GN).

inhabited this territory for only two centuries. Their tradition, which they called the "ancient word," held that their ancestors were born in the region of Anáhuac, toward the setting sun; white men, or fire warriors, had reached their shores on floating villages; with them their ancestors had become allied, and together they had invaded the old Cacique empire, which they had successfully subjugated.[8] Then the conquerors were attacked in their turn; forced to choose between exile and enslavement, they had fled to the banks of the Mississippi. The Natchez still cultivated their sense of proud independence, which grew all the more uncompromising in their new home in the forest wilderness. They were indomitable against all save their chieftains, referred to as "suns," who were the objects of fanatical devotion, as the following anecdote illustrates.

In 1716 some Canadians and two Frenchmen were descending the Mississippi when some Natchez, under orders of one of their chiefs, attacked and killed them. Bienville boldly went to demand that he be given the head of the assassin. The Natchez replied that the guilty person was a "sun" and therefore inviolate. Bienville stood his ground and issued threats. Then one Indian resolved to die for his chief; his head was severed and presented to Bienville as being that of the "sun." Bienville learned of the substitution and declared it unsatisfactory. A second victim offered himself, in the hope of being more acceptable than the first: a vain deceit! Only after the failure of this double sacrifice did the Natchez resign themselves to delivering up the guilty one and thus to becoming guilty themselves of sacrilege.

The distrust first felt by the Chickasaws had already spread to the Natchez when the construction of Fort Rosalie gave fresh grounds for their resentment. This military post provoked such protests that [Boucher de la] Périer, the successor of Bienville at the head of the government of Louisiana, requested that the Compagnie d'Occident send some reinforcements. The request was denied. Matters progressively

---

[8] According to Gayarré, the "white men on floating villages" were Cortez and the *conquistadores*; the "old Cacique empire" was the Aztec empire of Mexico (Gayarré, *History,* p. 287).

worsened until finally, in 1729, a harsh act of injustice committed by the commander of Fort Rosalie set off an explosion of the hatreds which had been silently brooding. The very existence of the colony as a whole, as well as that of the fort, was jeopardized on this occasion.

The commander, who needed to develop a large agricultural district, judged that no location was better suited to the purpose than the village of Pomme, inhabited by a tribe of Natchez. Instead of negotiating with them and at least finding out if they could be peacefully relocated, he summoned their chief and ordered that the town be cleared of all inhabitants without delay. In a vain effort to prevent this usurpation, the Indian chief spoke these simple and affecting words:

When you and your brothers first came and asked for land, we granted it to you; we had enough for you and ourselves. The same sun shone on both our peoples, the same land might sustain us both, receive our dead, and pass on to our children. Why then deprive us of the fields and forests we share with you, the cabins to which we have welcomed you, the mat upon which we have sat to smoke the peace pipe with you?

The blind rage of the commander was neither assuaged nor enlightened.[9] His only concession was to delay the brutal dispossession until after the harvest was completed; in return for the granting of this delay, he would exact a tribute of grain. The embittered Natchez resolved to obtain for themselves a tribute of blood. Their great fathers were convoked in a council, at which the extermination of the French was advocated, not only the murder of those who had particularly oppressed them, but a general massacre to rid the soil of all its invaders. The plan was submitted to the overlord, or Great Sun of the Natchez, who ratified it and transmitted it not only to the chiefs of the tribes under his command, but to the neighboring tribal leaders as well. All adopted it; driven by a common hatred, they joined forces for a com-

---

[9] "His name was Chepar" (GN). Gayarré's *History,* p. 396, fails to give this spelling, but lists variations of the name as Chopart, Chépart, and Etcheparre. Gaillardet's spelling is closer to that used by Chateaubriand, in whose work, *Les Natchez* (published 1826), the French commander figures prominently and is named Chépar.

mon vengeance. To set the date, the Natchez made fagots and distributed them to every village. Each fagot contained exactly the same
number of reeds. Beginning on the day when the moon should be new,
the people were to remove one reed per evening from their fagot;
when only one remained, it would become the signal and symbol of the
attack.

The fatal day drew near, and what a remarkable as well as terrible
fact that, among so many diverse and heretofore mutually hostile
tribes, not one man spoke to divulge the secret of this conspiracy of the
Indian nations united in a single body and in a single crusade against
their oppressors! The secret of this mysterious, firmly planted alliance
had to fall upon a woman's ear for it to pass across lips to betray it.
The woman was the wife of a chieftain or "sun." As a young maiden
she had had an intimate relationship with a Frenchman; through him
she had conceived a love for the whole race. Her observant eye suggested to her that the Indians were involved in some important plot;
in a woman, suspicion must resolve into certainty. She lured one of her
sons away into the woods, there reproached him for not properly con-
fiding in his mother, and succeeded in extracting his secret from him.

The fagot of reeds sent to her village was housed in the temple of
the Great Sun. As her rank gave her access to this holy place, the ten-
der-hearted Indian matron went in on various occasions and removed
some of the reeds, which she cast into the fire so as to upset entirely
the plan for concerted action. She was not content merely to have
divided the massacre in two. Knowledge of the great secret made her
feel torn between conflicting interests, her fondness for the enemy and
her loyalty to her own people. She could not bring herself to the glory
or shame of a direct revelation, but she knew of the love that some
young Indian maids of her acquaintance were experiencing for certain
Frenchmen, how they echoed her own tender sentiments of an earlier
day. It was to these girls that she divulged the secret, confident that it
would reach the ears of those most deeply concerned. The woman was
not mistaken. The lovers of the Indian girls, being informed by them,
went straight to the commander of the fort with the news. This officer's

stupidity was, however, to destroy these men whose lives had already been jeopardized by his harshness. He received the report with scornful disbelief, accused those who delivered it of cowardice, and threw them into prison.

On November 28, 1729, Indians appeared from all sides at the fort. Each carried his share of the grain which was expected as the tribute levied against them. They were therefore admitted without suspicion. While they moved freely within the stockade and to the residence of the commander himself, others spread about the countryside and stationed themselves as deadly sentinels in each town, at each house, by each citizen. At the signal, consisting of a volley of rifle fire from the top of the fort, the raised blades struck down, and the general massacre was accomplished forthwith. Of the 700 people who lived in that colony, the only ones whose lives were spared were 150 children, 80 adult women who served as slaves, and a few Negro men who were plantation laborers. The entire district was subjected to plundering and murder. At the time when this homicidal task was being carried out, the narratives state that the Great Sun of the Natchez smoked his pipe in calm. His men brought him the heads of the officers—that of the fort commander he kept beside him; all the rest were placed around the walls of his room.

After the taste of blood came that of strong drink. A savage orgy, accompanied by dancing and whooping, went on for several days and several nights as well, by the light of the fires.

A fort that we had built in the Yazoo country was similarly attacked and its inhabitants similarly beheaded. The bloodshed would have been unending if it had not been for the clever Indian woman's trickery in advancing the date for concerted action. When other tribes involved in the conjuration learned of the premature massacres, several refused to follow suit, considering that they had been betrayed and that the French, being now forewarned, were also forearmed. In New Orleans a Negro conspiracy, which was in all likelihood a ramification of the Natchez plot, was disclosed in time.

Word of this horrible tragedy struck the people of New Orleans with grief and indignation. General Périer determined to inflict a smashing counterblow. Because his forces were insufficient he negotiated an alliance with the Choctaw Indians. Their braves were put on the warpath while a corps of three hundred French troops prepared to join them, under the command of Major Loubois.[10] The Natchez had destroyed Fort Rosalie, and, from its wreckage and the weapons seized, they had constructed in another district a new fort of their own, defended by several lines of palisades. The French and Choctaw fighters surrounded and laid siege to it. On March 25, 1730, the Natchez sent word that they were ready to surrender; they offered to return all the prisoners they had captured provided the besiegers would withdraw to the Mississippi shore; in case of a refusal, they warned that they were prepared to burn the captives. The rescue of these captives was paramount in the minds of the besiegers. Loubois retreated to the place stipulated; the women, children, and Negro slaves were released to him. Taking advantage of his withdrawal, and under cover of darkness, the Natchez departed, evacuating their fort. The following day Loubois returned to find nothing there but deserted huts. He destroyed the Indian entrenchments, rebuilt Fort Rosalie, stationed a garrison in it, and returned to New Orleans with the liberated women, children, and slaves.

This was not, however, the end of the struggle between the colonists and the Natchez. The latter, emboldened over having escaped from the siege, were relentlessly brash, both in spirit and in destructive act. Incidents in which entire teams of forest workers were captured and slain, houses pillaged, and travelers robbed gave repeated evidence of their continued presence even in the vicinity of Fort Rosalie, incidents that hastened preparations for a new offensive against them. The Indians learned of these preparations and at last decided to abandon these regions and withdraw to the plateau separating the Red and Arkansas River basins from the western side of the Mississippi. This

[10] "Loubois was rewarded for his successful campaign against the Natchez by being appointed Major and Commander of New Orleans" (Gayarré, *History*, p. 435).

natural barrier between our colonists and them would, they thought, constitute sufficient protection.

Meanwhile, the Compagnie d'Occident had suffered heavy losses from the recent Natchez uprisings; with no profitable operations in sight for itself and with its reputation fast sinking, it decided to give up the colony for which it had lost all hope. It carried in its composition the same fatal flaw that had killed Crozat's company—I refer to the principle of monopoly. In 1730 it relinquished to the King all rights which had been granted it. The court retained Périer as governor of Louisiana and sent some troops there at his insistence. The determined executive was more than ever intent on crushing the Natchez, in retaliation for their disregard of French laws and the laws of humanity. He set forth in the middle of winter, went up the Mississippi, the Red River, and the Black River, beginning a search for the Natchez, who had gone into hiding deep in a forest wilderness. Perhaps their abode would not have been discovered except that by chance a young Indian was found fishing, who, in taking flight, revealed the path which led to the main encampment of his people. The boy was captured before he could complete his escape, and on January 20, 1731, the Natchez were suddenly attacked. Their position was fortified, and they proved to be prepared to defend it. They even made a few daring raids to halt the construction of our trenches. Then a bomb landed inside their fort in the enclosure reserved for their women and children, setting off woeful cries and riotous panic. The Indians signaled for a cease-fire and a chance to surrender. Périer demanded that their chiefs come to his camp for a peace talk. They refused to comply until it was clear that it was their last recourse, and they had no sooner reached the conference room than they changed their minds and tried to escape. They pretended to fall into deep sleep; one of them in this way succeeded in fleeing past their unsuspecting guards. When he reached his own camp, he reported that there was no hope of clemency on the part of the French. Therefore, when Périer sent them an ultimatum they rejected it, announcing that they did not fear death and that he might resume his fire. This boast was a feint: they hoped to escape by night as they had before. Recourse to the same expedients again and again was a characteristic of the savage mentality; their cleverest stratagems were always marked by a measure of primitive simplicity. This time the French were on the alert—the runaways were halted, hemmed in, and forced back to the fort, which was to be their tomb. The majority of them perished; only a few were successful in their escape during a dark and stormy night; a small number surrendered unconditionally. These were brought back to New Orleans as slaves: the females were distributed to the various households, the males deported to Santo Domingo.

The Great Sun was one of the prisoners. Those who managed to escape were too small a number to reorganize themselves under another chief, and sought refuge among the Chickasaws, their predecessors in revolt, asking to be adopted as members of their tribe. This right of asylum was a commonly accepted custom among the American aborigines and assured the newcomers of absolute protection. "The land of our fathers is overrun," explained the petitioners, "fire has devoured our forests, homes, and crops; our weapons are all we have left. Grant that we may live with you, share your burdens, and fight your enemies."

The Chickasaws granted the adoption requested by the Natchez, and into their society disappeared this savage people, the most highly civilized tribe of Louisiana, where they would now be forgotten were it not for the flourishing new city which has adopted their name as a link with the distant past.

CHAPTER NINE

Members of the New Orleans Bar

NEW YORK, FEBRUARY 13, 1840—The New Orleans bar includes in its membership a number of remarkable men; regrettably the limited space of a newspaper article prevents an attempt at a character sketch of each one. We shall therefore choose, from among this group of luminaries, just four names at the top of a distinguished list, these four being worthy of special consideration because of the high place to which public opinion has assigned them. These outstanding men are Messrs. Mazureau and Pierre Soulé of the French bar and Messrs. Preston and Grymes of the American bar.

Monsieur Mazureau occupies in New Orleans the eminent position of attorney general.[1] Born in France, he experienced in his career the changes of fortune which were the lot of men and nations at the end of the last century and the beginning of the present century. Mazureau served in the French Navy at the time of several of our glorious naval engagements, which he witnessed as an active participant. Piously faithful to those noble memories, he loves to reminisce about that

---

[1] Étienne Mazureau (1777–1849) arrived in New Orleans in 1804; he became attorney general in 1815. See Edward L. Tinker, "Mazureau, Étienne," in *Dictionary of American Biography.*

period of his life. Mazureau remembers; he feels honored to have once worn the uniform of the French Navy.

His character has been, moreover, to a large extent stamped by that background. Mazureau has kept the ebullient, energetic seaman's viewpoint while draped in his magistrate's robe. His oratory owes to his earlier station in life its frank, virile, forthright quality. He affronts every prejudice squarely, accosts every vice like an enemy vessel that he boards with dagger in hand. His approach is direct and unhampered by formalism; his voice is vibrant and bold. One senses, in listening to him, that here is a man both conscious of his persuasive powers and conscientious in his use of them. His legal knowledge is profound, for his training has been rigorous and tenacious. His knowledge is deeper than it is wide, however; it appears to be centrally focussed rather than far-reaching. Mazureau is a specialist: with noble modesty, he freely admits this limitation. After such an admission, one must judge him rather self-contradictory in harboring the most opinionated, brutal, and unswerving prejudices against certain men and certain schools of thought. I have heard Mazureau refer to the scientist Orfila as a worthless scoundrel and to Victor Hugo as a spineless marionette.[2] Mazureau is a confirmed classicist. Practically every work or personality of a modern tendency has sometime or other appeared in the dock of the accused during his rambling digressions. Almost always he conducts the trial of literature along with the trial of the criminal.

When he is engaged in a legal debate his reasoning is ironclad and his logic of granite strength, so long as he sticks to legal precedents and their consequences. When based upon a syllogism, his argumentation is irrefutable. It becomes shakier when based on evidence. In that realm he finds moving sands with no longer a firm foundation. The help of a legal text is to Mazureau's speech what ballast is to a ship.

[2] Mathieu Orfila (1787–1853), scientist and physician, dean of the Faculty of Medicine, Paris, author of works on toxicology and legal medicine. Gaillardet suggests that Mazureau's conservatism refused to accept Orfila's medical theories any more than Hugo's revolutionary literary ideas. Gaillardet's faint praise of Mazureau, as compared with that which he heaped upon Soulé, is explained in part by their conflicting viewpoints on current literature.

Without the extra weight it drifts and flounders after having been so smooth and sure. When this happens Mazureau has an irresistible tendency toward bombast. His speech rises higher and higher, and, like a balloon, the higher it rises, the less there is in it. Such flights of oratory are followed by abrupt descents. His speech tends to be tightly strung: as long as reason, the balancing pole of the mind, is firmly grasped, he proceeds with aplomb through his speech; but when the balancing pole is dropped he falls grotesquely. For him, there is less than a step from the sublime to the ridiculous. His ringing tones, large flaming eyes, and powerful head couched in a thick neck suggest a Mirabeau or a hobgoblin by turns, depending on the felicitous or infelicitous inspiration of the moment. He terrifies, or he is ludicrous. His admirable harangues and his incredible incongruities are equally memorable.

Mazureau is one of the strongest pillars of the social structure of New Orleans. Society relies upon him in confidence. He is the Archidamus of criminal law.[3] Woe unto the guilty party who must grapple with this powerful adversary! An accusation has never fallen into Mazureau's hands without his wringing it dry of every drop of punishment that may be extracted from it. When on the track of a crime he will catch its scent, follow its traces, hound it, and not let up until it is at bay. If the defense then tries to rob him of his prey, it is a sight to see him muster all his strength and back up against the law, his lair! A sight to see him harassed by a pack of defense attorneys, bristling his mane and snorting into the fray! Mazureau is the prosecution incarnate, a walking requisitory. This relentless high priest of the law honors his ministry with all the inflexibility, but also all the impartiality, which ennoble and sanctify this holy calling.

The American lawyer Preston[4] is equally distinguished as a member

[3] Of the several Spartan kings who bore this name, Archidamus III (ca. 403–338 B.C.) may be identified as the one to whom reference is here made. He is credited with the winning of the battle of Midea against the Argives and the Arcadians, at which ten thousand of the enemy perished without the loss of a single Spartan. Mazureau's legal triumphs in New Orleans were comparably decisive.

[4] Isaac Trimble Preston (1793–1852), educated at Yale and Litchfield Law

of the legislature and as a member of the Louisiana bar. I shall not
enter upon any analysis of his oratorical skill, as my insufficient knowledge of the language precluded my competence to judge of it. What
I could observe and affirm is that a great part of the effectiveness of
this lawyer in the courtroom stems from the contrast between his facial
expression and his vocal expression. Preston was endowed by nature
with the plainest, most undistinguished face one could see anywhere.
When that face appears at the bar, many a juryman wonders if the late
George Dandin has not come back to life.[5] Once this outwardly common fellow begins to speak, once this normally calm, slow voice warms
up and gains forcefulness, once this broad goose's head lights up, becomes alert and active, then beneath the previously dull, now lively
brow, one sees the gleam of the eagle's gaze. The metamorphosis is
total. The observer who has witnessed the phases of this transfiguration
and has been gripped in bemused fascination is now swept away with
him on his sovereign flight.

Examples of such a deceptive outward appearance, a kind of mask by
which the physical man disguises and conceals the moral man, are not
so rare as one might think. The annals of literature offer more than
one case in point, after that of wonderful La Fontaine, whose exquisitely delicate intellect was hidden beneath such a forbidding outer
crust that people were amazed that he could be the poet of the immortal fables.[6]

Preston's rival at the bar and on the platform, Lawyer Grymes,[7] is

---

School, made his reputation in New Orleans as a lawyer and became a judge
of the Supreme Court of Louisiana.

[5] In Molière's play *George Dandin* the title character personifies the naïve
bewilderment of the bourgeois trying to come to terms with an overrefined aristocracy.

[6] The best known physical description of Jean de La Fontaine, to which Gaillardet here alludes, is that by La Bruyère, the appropriate lines of which we
translate as follows: ". . . seems crude, heavy, stupid; he cannot talk, cannot
even relate what he has just now seen" (*Les Caractères*, chapter entitled "Des
Jugements").

[7] John Randolph Grymes, Jr. (1786–1854), like Mazureau, served both as
attorney general of Louisiana and as a member of the state legislature. He

one whose talents and powers are plainly imprinted in his physique: a tall erect body, penetrating eyes, and an icy and aloof expression. He is the Anglo-Saxon gentleman, phlegmatic, politely reserved, shedding his sternness only when among his peers, or to show gallantry to a lady, or to jest at the foibles of one and all. Lawyer Grymes obeys his most passionate impulses with coldness; he would win or lose a fortune without batting an eyebrow. Several years ago, the president of one of the branches of the Louisiana legislature fell into serious trouble with him and decided to refuse him the satisfaction he demanded. Grymes got out a pistol and coolly proceeded to the Capitol, determined to blow the brains out of his antagonist. The latter was informed in advance and therefore armed himself also. An exchange of shots at close range ensued between the two parties. One of Lawyer Grymes's arms was shattered. "Didn't you know your adversary was expecting you?" one of his friends asked him later.

"Certainly I knew it," was the reply, "but what difference should that have made?"

A bill collector in New Orleans who was supposed to collect a debt from Lawyer Grymes had been unsuccessful after repeated efforts to dun him. "Sir," he appealed to him at last in woeful tones, "you are making me wear out more shoes than my commissions can pay for."

"I can well imagine," answered the lawyer; "here then are two dollars to get your shoes repaired, and I'll give you a like amount every month from now on."

Along with this stoical disposition and ironic tendency, Lawyer Grymes has a scepticism on matters of the soul that is highly amusing or afflicting, depending upon the convictions of the one who is to be his judge. He professes every kind of atheism—moral, social, and religious. Sparing no one, he freely displays his opinions; he is the first

---

received Pierre Soulé hospitably when the latter first arrived in New Orleans late in 1825. Gayarré includes a sketch of Grymes in his "Louisiana Bench and Bar in 1823," pp. 889–900. The anecdote of the bill collector is repeated there, as well as Grymes's affectation of unpreparedness in court and his boastful unorthodoxy, among other traits.

to accuse himself and those who share his scepticism, and thus to steal
the fire of others who might take pleasure in condemning him. Doubt
is his only faith, and he proclaims it with careless frankness. His argu-
ments on the subject are characterized by unashamed assuredness and
were unabated until a simple woman asked a simple question: "Would
you dare profess and defend such doctrines before your own child?"
This woman was his wife. The philosopher in him was silenced, and
gave way to the father.

To have described the man is to have described the lawyer. The good
and bad qualities of the one have necessarily impinged upon the other.
His chief assets are his reasoning power and his use of language; he
handles words with rare dexterity. He appears in the judicial arena like
a gladiator armed to the teeth, relying only upon his own resources,
believing, one can imagine, in no other justice than success. He draws
strength from his egotism and zeal from his very incredulity. A favorable verdict: in this is his trust, the only god to whom he will pay
homage or voice prayer. Lawyer Grymes is, on the other hand, almost
as noted for his laziness as for his ability. He has often been seen to
appear at a trial without any previous study of the case he is to defend.
He listens to all other lawyers who may be there to speak, and from the
raw material of their remarks he constructs his defense. Out of a hovel,
he can build a palace, if need be. His active mind absorbs the words
of the others, assimilates them, and creates from their contents a whole
new edifice.

Of the four names I mentioned to start with, I have yet to speak of
Lawyer Soulé, of the French side of the bar. The addition of his name
will be enough to tip the scales decisively in that direction.

Soulé is the king of the Louisiana bar. The wide scope of his abilities
and the complex virtues of his oratory have won for him this uncontested and incontestable crown. The men whom we have previously
sketched are smart, effective lawyers; Soulé is more than a lawyer, he
is an orator. He always sees beyond the case he is defending; he always
seeks out and expounds more than mere law—I mean the philosophy
of law. His own high standards are those of reason, the natural law

which is over and above the written law. Consequently, critics who are unable to grasp the loftiness of his intellect think that they are pointing to a flaw when they say he is poor at chicanery. His synthetic mind joyfully dives from cause to effect and soars from consequences to governing principles; quite the reverse of the pettifogger whose legalistic scalpel plays on the epiderm of the law to extract its dead letter, he resuscitates the corpse, animates it with his breath, and questions its spirit. Far from trailing slavishly in the wake of his case, like those breathless litigants who tie themselves to the judicial harness to sweat blood and water, he whisks his hearers along after him in a perpetually free and impetuous course, never stopping to release them until they are giddy, dazed, and overwhelmed by his tremendous drive and irresistible genius.

Soulé's qualities, in their totality, offer a dual contrast with those of Mazureau and those of Grymes. The eloquence of the latter two is materialistic, to a certain extent; Soulé's is entirely spiritual. When Mazureau cites a text to him, he retorts by citing reason; when Grymes plays upon words, he plays upon the heartstrings. His speech always flows warmly and abundantly; a sort of fervor animates and inspires it. Grymes and Soulé are Protestantism and Catholicism oratorically exemplified. Theirs are the voices of doubt and faith. The contrasting qualities of their native tongues, in producing a difference of form, emphasize the difference in content.

Soulé possesses, however, a remarkable mastery of the American language; steadfast work and stubborn determination have rewarded him with control of the harsh, foreign sounds. His voice is rich; its vibrant tones rise and fall with incredible expressiveness. He is sober of gesture, noble and unaffected in appearance. A fine head, over which projects the dark profundity of his hair and his thoughts; a broad brow, the receptacle of a vast intelligence; piercing eyes, whose searching gaze rises obliquely upon its object and encompasses it totally; open-hearted generosity and friendliness of manner, the outward signs of a heart of gold and a highly cultivated background: there, in a nutshell, is the portrait of Pierre Soulé.

His story, or rather, that of the causes which cast such a richly endowed talent upon the American shore, deserves to be told.

In the last years of the Restoration, Soulé was a young lawyer of Paris, who edited and contributed to the newspaper *Le Nain,* the successor to *Le Nain Jaune,* which had been stifled some time previously under the pressure of repeated adverse court decisions. The new *Nain* had inherited all the malice and destructive wit of its late parent. Its fortunes and growth were in the hands of a group including those two literary brothers from Marseilles, Barthélemy and Méry, twin stars who appeared together in the Restoration literary heavens; the lawyer Ledru-Rollin; Léon Halévy; and a few other young men whose names became known later in various fields and whose fame has often reached the ears of their former associate Pierre Soulé, whereas they may well have remained ignorant of what became of him.[8]

In the year 1825 Soulé had the rash impulse to put into the mouth of the satirical *Nain* a politico-literary squib in which the smooth-cheeked stripling gave all the outstanding graybeards of the day a sound lashing with the whip of his patriotic indignation. This lampooning annoyed the public prosecutor to such an extent that he obtained for its author a fine of ten thousand francs and a two-year prison term. Thus condemned, our hero recalled the lines:

> Cruel fortune, though I lose,
> I'll not pay up unless I choose![9]

Instead of sacrificing his liberty in payment of his debt to the state, he chose exile. He was offered a chance for a secretarial position in a

---

[8] Auguste-Marseille Barthélemy (1796–1867) and Joseph Méry (1798–1865) collaborated on bitterly satirical literary works. Alexandre-Auguste Ledru-Rollin (1807–1874) became a member of the Chamber of Deputies in 1841 (one year after the present chapter was published), and continued to be active in French politics until his death. Léon Halévy (1802–1883), a younger brother of the composer Fromental Halévy (*La Juive*), was equally gifted as a poet, dramatist, and historian; his son, Ludovic Halévy, was the librettist of Bizet's *Carmen* and of numerous operas by Offenbach.

[9] The original French for these verses is a slight misquotation of two lines of Jean-François Regnard's *Le Joueur,* Act I, Scene IV.

South American republic; he sailed to England, heavy of heart and light of purse. On his arrival in Liverpool, he was told that the position he was seeking had just been granted to some one else who had already set sail to occupy it. Soulé thus found himself penniless, friendless, and homeless on foreign soil. Faced with a choice between two incarcerations and two poverties, he reasoned that incarceration and poverty on his home ground would be preferable. Having decided to give himself up to the French prison authorities, he sailed back to Le Havre without delay. As he stepped ashore, the first person he encountered was a man who, like himself, had fallen into disfavor with the Restoration. This was Admiral Baudin, then a mere merchant with an office on the square in Le Havre. He intercepted Soulé, vividly pointed out to him the risks he would run in giving himself up, revived his faltering spirits, led him to a ship he himself was about to send off to Santo Domingo, and offered him a choice between the darkness of prison on the one hand and the light of liberty on the other. The condemned lad jumped aboard and sailed away, carrying with him as his only baggage a few letters of recommendation—and new hope.

A Frenchman who was in business in Port-au-Prince and another from New Orleans both advised him, on his reaching his destination, that he should continue on as far as Louisiana. There he would find welcome reminders of the old country among the Creole population and also some chance of making a living as a lawyer. Soulé followed this advice.[10] A knowledge and practice of the English language was essential to the realization of his ambitions. Soulé immediately sequestered himself in the western territories, cut himself off from all French contacts, and forced himself to deal exclusively with American speakers. He dug his ravenous teeth into their tough language, chewed it, and digested it with all the avidity of a man driven by a double hunger, for bread and knowledge.

For a time, his financial straits were such that he was obliged to seek

[10] Before reaching New Orleans he made stops in Haiti, Baltimore, and New York (Amos Aschbach Ettinger, *The Mission to Spain of Pierre Soulé, 1853–1855: A Study in the Cuban Diplomacy of the United States,* p. 105).

employment as a manual laborer. He applied at the door of a monastery and there was hired as a gardener.[11]

Some friends in New Orleans found out indirectly about his uncomplainingly accepted poverty and came to his rescue. They located him just in time, for he was flat on his back with illness of body and mind on a poor boardinghouse bed in Louisville.

No sooner had he recovered than Soulé was back in New Orleans to dare to plead his first case in English. He had devoted five months to extensive and concentrated study, under the constant fomentation of solitude and deprivation: the result was a rapid rise of fortune. A year before I met him, Pierre Soulé was the foremost lawyer of New Orleans, as measured by his ability and his clientele. He had, through the magical power and sublime charity of his words, saved a hundred or more poor devils from death or infamy. He was married to a young Creole beauty: this crowning good fortune afforded him his greatest pride and the greatest envy of others. He was one of the political and financial leaders of New Orleans and the president of one of the leading banks. He had endowed his adopted state with the finest architectural structure it possesses.[12] In short, he had been for ten years the worthiest personification of France in America. Then he made plans to return to France and enjoy the fruits of his labors. The district of his birthplace, which had never ceased to profit from his generosity even after his prison sentence and self-banishment, now awaited and solicited the return of the ex-journalist native son, so that he might be elected a representative to the National Assembly. When the people of Louisiana heard that they were about to lose from their midst this

[11] The job was at the Dominican Monastery in Bardstown, Kentucky. His diary and a letter of this period are preserved in the collections of the Louisiana State Historical Society, New Orleans (Ettinger, *Mission to Spain,* p. 106).

[12] In 1828 he was married to Armantine Mercier, of a prominent family of New Orleans (Ettinger, *Mission to Spain,* pp. 106–107). The "finest architectural structure" was the New Orleans Exchange. Soulé was appointed a director of a building association for the eighth district of New Orleans in 1834. The charter for the building of the Exchange is dated 1835. On February 12, 1839, the building was destroyed by fire (John F. Condon, "Annals of Louisiana," in François Xavier Martin, *The History of Louisiana,* pp. 436, 438, 442).

distinguished guest, they financed by public subscription a bust in his likeness; they obtained his permission that it be placed in the main hall of the Stock Exchange, the building for which New Orleans had him to thank. Everything was in readiness for the departure: he had disposed of his home and property; passage aboard a steamship was reserved for him and his family; his thoughts were already dwelling on his native shore once more. Suddenly, all these castles in the air of patriotic devotion crumbled at his feet.

We do not feel at liberty to mention the details of this disaster, out of respect for others involved, whom our pen has no right to name and to accuse; suffice it to say that Soulé's collapse was a result of the noblest feeling of confidence that could be born of the noblest sense of gratitude. In the eyes of God or man, such a downfall is more admirable than the most spectacular rise to success![13]

Pierre Soulé remained in New Orleans. There, astride the ruins of his past, he set about rebuilding his future. Impoverished as far as wealth in gold is concerned, he is commonly regarded as richer than ever in the wealth that comes from the respect and devotion of his fellow man. Therefore, the Democratic Party of Louisiana, of which he was one of the strongest supporters, has conceived the intention of taking him as its leader. Soulé has agreed to accept the candidacy for this demanding office, the perilous honor of which he had previously declined to consider. Louisiana will then probably have its own Berryer in government as well as at the bar.[14] In this position Soulé

[13] Gaillardet here refers to Soulé's loss of fortune and to his conduct following the panic of 1837: "Wide distress evoked his generosity and affected his own fortunes to the extent that he lost or gave away well-nigh his entire wealth, necessitating a renewed struggle for affluence" (Ettinger, *Mission to Spain*, pp. 107–108). Gaillardet's own finances suffered considerably during this crisis, and Soulé's generosity must have extended to our author, his brother, and others associated in the wine-importing business which they were attempting to establish in New Orleans (cf. J. Fromageot, "Un Tonnerrois 'éruptif' de l'époque romantique," *L'Écho d'Auxerre*, no. 56 (mars–avril, 1965), pp. 24–27).

[14] Pierre-Antoine Berryer (1790–1868) aided his father in the defense of Marshal Ney and subsequently obtained the acquittal of other Napoleonic of-

will be greater than ever: for his thoughts will be focussed on a wider horizon; for his oratorical genius has been sharpened by the grinding of adversity and has acquired new power and range. Before, his outstanding ability was his command of the emotions of his listeners; today, he commands a sort of veneration. To all the crowns that adorned his brow, Soulé has added that of misfortune, and this is the holiest crown of all.

Now, to bring to an end this incomplete survey of the Louisiana bar, I must mention the name of a prince who for a time had a place on the roster. Achille Murat, the son of the former King of Naples, made a start as a lawyer of New Orleans, and his start demonstrated that he was, if not an orator, a most remarkable man. For some strange reason, which was not the only strange thing about his character, the citizen-prince did not follow up this first attempt; he has since left both the profession and the continent.[15] I shall therefore confine myself to the relation of a single anecdote which marked his short sojourn in this land. Its accuracy is vouchsafed by the poet Méry, who heard it from the lips of the Princess of Lipona, the mother of Prince Achille. It is a touching story, the first chapter of which takes us back to the dawn of the Empire, the concluding one to the time of the July Revolution.

In the days when Italy was a French province, a military mutiny broke out in the garrison of Leghorn. The mutiny was serious enough to awaken in the anger of Emperor Napoleon. As he would brook no insubordination, he resolved to quench this flare-up before it could spread any farther, and to inflict exemplary punishment upon the guilty, so as to strike terror into the hearts of any other soldiers tainted with the contagion of revolt. Joachim Murat was given the painful duty of carrying out this stringent measure; he departed at once for

---

ficers. Later, he was equally prominent in politics as well, being elected to the National Assembly in 1830. He was considered to be the greatest parliamentary and legal orator of the nineteenth century in France.

[15] Murat went to Europe in 1839 to settle the estate of his mother; he remained there almost without interruption for the remaining five years of his life (cf. A. J. Hanna, *A Prince in Their Midst: The Adventurous Life of Achille Murat on the American Frontier*, pp. 222–223).

Leghorn. When he reached the town, the rebellion had died of itself; sorrow and shame had taken the place of a passing resentment in the emotions of the soldiers. A fatal example had nonetheless been set, and the Emperor's orders gave him no alternative: he must exact the punishment.

Murat convoked the soldiers of the garrison, rebuked them harshly for their bad conduct, and commanded that they denounce to him the instigators of the revolt. If they failed to comply, ten men would be chosen at random from each battalion to face the firing squad. The soldiers, with bowed heads, expressed their willingness to accept whatever expiation their Emperor's mercy might require, but they pleaded with his general not to impose upon them the shameful role of informing, for that would result in the punishment of a few for a crime of which all were guilty. Murat remained inflexible, and ten men chosen by lot were about to be brought forward from the ranks, when three men voluntarily advanced and announced that they alone were responsible for the first outbreak of mutiny. The remorse of these temporarily wayward soldiers was so genuine, so touchingly expressed; the brows of these tried-and-true soldiers were so furrowed with grief and regret; their eyes, which never before had been lowered, were so painfully downcast—Murat could not repress his deep emotion. He hesitated, fell silent, and then finally ordered that the three guilty ones be thrown into a cell to await their execution on the morrow.

Late in the evening of this sad day, while the city slept and the silence of the night was unbroken except for the measured footsteps of the patrols marching through the empty streets or the occasional cry of the sentinel from atop the ramparts: "Who goes there?" Murat sat in his bedchamber with the three men before him, holding their caps in their hands, crying like little children, the tears rolling down their drooping mustaches. Death was not what they feared, these veterans of Arcole and Marengo, but the shameful death of traitors. For life they had no regrets, but only for their fault.

"Listen carefully," said Murat, "I am convinced of your true repentance and want to save you. Tomorrow, at break of day, you will be led to the place of military execution, outside the city walls. There will be no spectators present, I shall see to that. The rifles will be fired; you will fall and remain motionless on the ground until the firing squad has left. A trusted friend will take you and place you inside a vehicle completely sealed up to avoid inspection. A ship sails tomorrow for America. You will be led aboard, suitably disguised. Meanwhile, here for each of you is a purse full of gold. Promise that you will always remain faithful to my trust."

The three men flung themselves to their general's feet and dampened them with their tears.

Things happened just as he had said. Napoleon himself was as unsuspecting as anyone else; he thanked Murat for having carried out his mission with the lives of only three men.

The story remained a secret closely guarded by those concerned until 1830, when Prince Achille Murat one day went walking in the environs of New Orleans. Being overtaken by a storm, he sought shelter against a torrential downpour at the nearest house in sight. It was a house of very unprepossessing appearance. One man and woman with their children were its only inhabitants. The man received him with an austere but not unkind expression and with that somewhat stiff manner that an ex-soldier never completely loses.

After a few minutes of trivial conversation, a silence ensued between Prince Achille Murat and his host. The latter, from his seat on the opposite side of the room, kept his eyes fixed upon the Prince in a strangely preoccupied way. For his part, the Prince spent his enforced idleness by a cursory inspection of his surroundings, as he dried himself before the modest fire. Suddenly, he arose with a start. He had been examining the crude paintings of the battles and generals of the Empire on the walls. Placed above all the rest, beneath a crown of laurels, was a double portrait of Murat as general and as king.

"Did you serve in the French Army?" Prince Achille asked his host.

"Yes, sir," replied the latter with some hesitation.

"Where and under which officer did you see action?"

"In Italy, under General Murat."

At the mention of his father's name, the son of the soldier-king felt a certain thrill spread through him. He held out his hand to his father's companion-in-arms and asked, "Would you tell me your name, my good man?"

"Claude Gérard. And you, sir, might I inquire . . .?"

"I am Achille Murat."

"So it is true! My eyes and my heart did not deceive me! You are the son of my general, my prince, and my savior! If I am alive today and am a husband and father, it is thanks to him, sir. Your father was like a god to me."

Then the old soldier, interrupting himself with frequent exclamations and benedictions addressed to the memory of Murat and to the presence of his son, related, in the disjointed way that his intense emotion dictated, the story that I have set down above. With tears in his eyes, the Prince listened, and as long as the story continued, the hands of the young and the old man remained clasped in a grip that neither would release.

After that day, Prince Achille, who was by nature rather nonconformist and unsociable, chose not to mingle much in society, but rather to wander about the countryside near New Orleans. The favorite destination of his rambles and the shelter most dear to him for his rests was the poor, humble dwelling of his father's old companion-in-arms, the veteran of the army of occupation of Italy.

CHAPTER TEN

French Memories of Texas: Champ d'Asile

LE CONSTITUTIONNEL, PARIS, AUGUST 22, 1841—Texas is a land discovered by the Spanish; two facts, however, spaced apart by more than a century in the annals of French history, link this land to France by melancholy memories.

It was in Texas that the first colonization effort, directed to Louisiana, went astray and foundered, after having been placed by Louis XIV under the the command of heroic, ill-fated La Salle. It was at Saint Bernard Bay (today Matagorda Bay) that La Salle landed with his disoriented colonizers; it was by La Salle that many streams were discovered: the Caney, the Lavaca, the Río Colorado (which he named the Rivière Rouge), the Sablonnière, the Maligne, the Trinity, and others, some of which have retained their original names in present-day Texas; it was on the banks of the Trinity, finally, near its western branch, that this man of wisdom and valor was killed by the hand of a Frenchman. There lie the bones of the sublime adventurer, lost in the wilderness; there strewn round him are those of his companions who fell beneath the savage tomahawk.

In 1815 the events before and after the date of March 20[1] had thrown the Imperial army into confusion and disunity. Numbers of officers and soldiers, their reputations ruined by their support of the defeated cause, foresaw a bleak future stretching before them. Their worst forebodings were soon realized by the order of proscription: on July 24 they were declared forever banished from their native soil. Thus hit by a law from which there was no appeal, the banished men determined to unite abroad and to seek a common refuge in their common misfortune. Thus was born the idea of the famous Champ d'Asile [literally, Field of Asylum]. It became a mecca not only for those struck by the political ban but also for many ex-soldiers, who suddenly found themselves jobless after an army career. Their only wealth was their bodily strength, their only activity was the display of courage; they resolved to seek out in the New World a subsistence and a home for their indigent glory.

Texas was chosen as the new home; yet by a strange oversight these exiles did not consult Spain to obtain a sanction for their settlement, although the place was one of its far-flung possessions. Spain's rule was, it is true, purely nominal and even contested to a certain degree by the United States; its own settlements were far from the intended site of the French colony and were swallowed up in the immense wilderness, where the actual sovereignty belonged to the savage Indians. However, despite Spain's apparent unconcern for its claim to these regions, as evidenced by their abandonment, it was not disposed to let them be usurped, as it later proved.

Texas had a well-deserved reputation for fertile soil and a healthy climate; it was the country closest to the United States, that new land of liberty, and to Louisiana, the former French territory. Here the remnants of the Empire might bask in their memories with a friendly power close at hand; here the glorious exiles might find a sanctuary for their unsettled lares and penates, a depository for their tattered banners.

[1] On March 20, 1815, Napoleon entered Paris, upon his return from Elba. This was the beginning date of the Hundred Days.

Undeniably, there was something grandiose and at the same time rather poignant in this plan for a Champ d'Asile. It was to be a colony of unprecedented origin and background, a family of the proscribed emerging from the great Imperial family and transporting itself with all its military aura onto American soil! A tomb for the mighty and a cradle of glory, this plot of ground called Champ d'Asile might become a nursery of future strength. Who could say what might spring from the ruins of such an illustrious past? If fortune had smiled upon the first efforts of our soldier-colonists, no flag anywhere on earth would have waved more hospitably to those thousands of emigrants who, for the past twenty years, have poured out of an over-crowded Europe. Thanks to a handful of its rejected children, France would thus have recovered a share of the vast American continent, of which its rivals, the English and Spanish races, today have exclusive possession. The consequences of a successful colonization would have been incalculable.

In the hands of France, Texas would today be the arbiter of America. As a close neighbor of Louisiana, the former French possession, where memories of the mother country might have been revived and fostered through neighborly contacts; rising like a column between that multi-armed giant the United States on the one hand, embracing more than two-thirds of North America, and, on the other, Mexico, already old while still in its infancy, weakened by its instability at a time when it should be at its strongest: Texas would have become a barrier for the one and a bulwark for the other. Its hands outstretched toward its two neighbors, it would have maintained an equilibrium between two unequal forces and would have arbitrated their rivalries. Such might have been the role of Texas, whose prosperous development under different auspices has survived the failure of Champ d'Asile, an ephemeral enterprise which hardly amounted to more than a daydream.

Let us add that, whereas the conception of Champ d'Asile may have been a noble and even fruitful idea when viewed in the broad perspective of French interests, it was also a kind of folly when viewed in the narrow perspective of the interests of the party which sponsored it.

Indeed, to remove so far from France the idle soldiers of the Empire, at a time when opposition to the Restoration government was mounting in the national consciousness, and to push to the opposite end of the earth these men accustomed to the use of force, restless veterans whose hands one might expect to need from one day to the next: this must be termed an egregious blunder on the part of the liberals and the Bonapartists. The Restoration sensed this, and therefore raised no objection to the emigration, which simply removed a thorn from its side. As for the liberals, their leaders soon realized their mistake in sacrificing a positive advantage to an adventurous gamble. If the founding of Champ d'Asile was, poetically speaking, a glorious thing, it was an untimely thing politically. This fact accounts for the sudden slackening of recruitment and fund raising that brought about the collapse of the colony, for it was built on too small a scale and was left exposed with few or no resources to withstand even the most ordinary tribulations with which its fragile foundation was soon undermined.

General Lallemand had been designated by the emigrants as commander in chief of the expedition; General Rigau was second in command.[2] Assembly points in New York and Philadelphia were set

[2] Baron Antoine Rigau (1758–1820), a hero of the battle of Austerlitz, was captured by the Russians in 1815 and became an exile in America in 1817. After participation in the expedition of Champ d'Asile, he returned to New Orleans, where he remained until his death.

General Charles Lallemand (1774–1839) was captured by the English after the battle of Waterloo and was detained for a time at Malta. Later he wandered through the Middle East before coming to America and organizing the project of Champ d'Asile. After his disappearance from the desperate scene at Galveston, one finds him briefly in Louisiana (1818–1819); Spain, Belgium, and France (1823); and New York, where he directed a school until 1830. His residence in the latter city was briefly interrupted by an altercation with Victor Jacquemont, the French naturalist, who was as intent upon a duel as Lallemand was to avoid one (1827–1828). In 1830 the government of Louis-Philippe permitted him to resume residence in France. He later became the military commander of the island of Corsica.

His middle names are variously given as Frédéric-Antoine (*Larousse; Webster's New International Dictionary*, 2nd ed.; *Encyclopedia Americana*) and as François-Antoine (*Dictionary of Universal Biography*, 2nd ed.; *Universal Pronouncing Dictionary of Biography and Mythology*, 5th ed.; *Appleton's Cyclo-*

for the participants. From these two ports the colonizers sailed to Texas; they were united on Galveston Island toward the middle of March, 1818, after suffering the loss of four men, who were swept away in a storm when within sight of the island of their destination. The center of the Champ d'Asile colony was established at approximately twenty leagues inland from the Gulf of Mexico on the banks of the Trinity River.

As soon as the supplies, munitions, and all other objects to be used by the colony were set ashore [state Hartmann and Millard, who were among the settlers of Champ d'Asile], we set to work building a temporary encampment and providing shelter against bad weather. Next, we were organized into platoons, Generals Lallemand and Rigau named the leaders of each. Once this organization was completed, plans were drawn up for four forts. One located to the right of our central camp was named Fort Charles in honor of the General in Chief; a second was named the Middle Fort; a third, Fort Henri, was located to the left and was to be connected by a covered walk to two guard posts placed within the camp. The fourth, located to the right of the camp enclosure and on the edge of the Trinity River, defended the shore and dominated the other three forts. It was named the Fort of the Stockade; it was to be fortified by three pieces of cannon; Fort Charles was to have two; the Middle Fort, one; and Fort Henri, two: a total of eight pieces of cannon to form our artillery.

These four forts were erected in short order, as if by magic. They were astonishingly well-built. The Fort of the Stockade was made of large tree trunks and was solid enough to have withstood any attack. The powder supply and tools of the colony were stored in it. Farther up from the forts and covering a rather wide area our dwellings were constructed in a circular formation. They were of large logs joined together in the form of bulletproof blockhouses with loopholes to have permitted house-to-house fighting if attacked. To the rear of center was General Lallemand's house; a short distance from it was the supply house; General Rigau's residence was lo-

---

pedia of American Biography, rev. ed.). For details on Lallemand's life, cf. Gilbert Chinard, "Les Expériences américaines de Victor Jacquemont," *Jacquemont*; Maurice Soulié, *Autour de l'aigle enchaîné: Le Complot du Champ d'Asile*.

cated behind Fort Henri near the two guard houses. The total effect of the camp was very pleasing: this rude, frontier scene had a kind of charm that was hard to imagine.

In one direction outside the camp was an enormous plain. In the opposite direction were evergreen trees, the tops of which were practically lost in the clouds. The right-hand boundary of the camp was formed by the Trinity River, which flowed on from our camp down to the Gulf of Mexico. On the opposite side of the river, forests stretched out as far as the eye could see. To the left and rear of the camp were also vast forests to protect us against storms.

During the periods of the day when work was not required, the colonists engaged in gardening; the very fertile land rewarded our labors beyond our expectations. Vegetation was very rapid; the area was soon covered with plants and fruit.

The colony was made up of four hundred persons, among whom numbered some foreigners, in particular some Spanish officers who had volunteered to join our emigrants.

The Indian tribes in the vicinity of the colonization area had greeted the palefaces with equanimity. Those of gentler character and more peaceable instincts even sent representatives to proffer the calumet of peace. These Indian delegates viewed the fortified camp with a mixture of curiosity and naïve admiration; an alliance was formed, cemented by an exchange of gifts, between General Lallemand and the Choctaws, Alabamas, Cochatis, and Tonkaways.

Everything thus seemed to point to the prosperity and development of the budding colony. The consequences of the initial error in the arrangements, however, were not long in manifesting themselves. It was learned that the Spanish garrisons of San Antonio and La Bahía, augmented by some Indian tribesmen, were advancing with the announced intention of forcing the withdrawal of the venturesome colony from land which it occupied without the authorization of the owners. This unexpected news caused General Lallemand to call a council meeting. The council was fearful that prolonged hostility might totally exhaust the limited supplies that the colony had on hand and therefore concluded that the wisest policy was to abandon the fortified camp, to remove from it the artillery and ammunition, and to retreat to the island of Galveston, which was the only point at which provisions could be obtained, since it was the only access to the sea.

As a result, no attempt was made to reach a peaceful settlement with the Spanish; the loss of such extensive work was no sooner resolved than consummated. The hapless, imprudent band of colonists took their place on the low, desert island, which possessed neither wood nor water supply. To obtain the latter, it was necessary first to dig deep cisterns; for food they could depend only upon their own stock of provisions with no hope of crops, no possibility of gardening. The consequence of this foolhardy, fatal move was soon evident: shortages began to appear. General Lallemand made up his mind to sail to New Orleans, there to seek help. He embarked, leaving the henceforth hopeless colony under the command of the elderly General Rigau, then close to his eightieth year.[3]

A few days after the departure of General Lallemand, a spokesman arrived from the Spanish commander who had taken possession of the abandoned Champ d'Asile. He delivered an order that the colonists withdraw from the island of Galveston. They replied that in the absence of their general in chief they could take no action and that they intended to await his return and to obey whatever orders he might issue. The spokesman departed, and the colonists, although stranded on this island, believed that they were at least free from external harassment. Cruel fortune intervened, however, to add its blows to the ineffectual ones of the Spanish.

Here I need only quote from the account by the witnesses of, and sufferers from, the catastrophe, Messrs. Hartmann and Millard.

Throughout our second stop at Galveston, the weather had been uniformly calm and mild, the temperature cool. It would have been an added

---

[3] Rigau died in his sixty-second year. This characteristic exaggeration of old age ends the first installment of the account of Champ d'Asile. The second half that follows was first published in the *Constitutionnel* one week later, August 29, 1841.

misfortune had turbulent weather occurred along with the forerunners of hunger and want which we faced. We had said as much from time to time, reasoning that fate was not entirely against us. We regarded our luck in this respect as a favorable omen, pointing to the eventual cessation of our present troubles which we felt so powerless to combat. We little dreamed that the storm was brewing overhead and that our previous misfortunes were as nothing compared to the blows which destiny was preparing to deliver, as if intent upon our utter destruction.

We were grouped at various points about our camp; the day was drawing to its close, the atmosphere was darkening, clouds accumulated, a wind rose, the seagulls were flying in to take shelter on land; in fact, every indication of an approaching storm was present before our eyes, yet far from being alarmed, we did not feel the slightest uneasiness. We believed that while inside our camp we were safe from any danger. Our entrenchments kept us out of the wind, and besides, our buildings were not tall enough to offer much chance of being swept away. As we had gone through similar perturbances before, we did not expect that this one would get any more violent. We were content to hammer down the stakes that seemed somewhat unsteady and to check the anchorage of our boats. Night soon shrouded the place in darkness; we all retired to our modest and humble abodes for our night's rest. We had already fallen into blissful slumber when suddenly we were aroused by the most startling noise. The wind blowing at its fiercest, the roar of the waves dashing against our entrenchments, and the lightning cracking through the clouds told us that nature was on the rampage. We were all the more terrified because the extraordinary darkness all about prevented us from making anything out; although the real danger was bad enough, it seemed to be a thousand times worse than it really was.

At last the swollen sea rolled its waves furiously over the entire island of Galveston. It penetrated our camp and our houses and flooded the whole. Soon we were surrounded by water four feet deep. Our excitement could not have been more intense. Cries of despair and suffering rang out to heighten the horror of this scene, but then they were drowned out by the unrestrained winds and waters, which sounded like the strongest cannon fire or the explosion of a mine. One may easily imagine how impatiently and anxiously we awaited the daylight through this eternal and terrible night, the immense disaster of which was magnified in our imaginations.

Day broke to reveal the extent of our losses and the abyss of waters about to swallow us up. We glanced about us with fear and terror. We dreaded to discover what our eyes would behold, yet we were overcome with curiosity. How painful was the sight! It was a picture of chaos, of destruction and of a disruption of nature whose laws seemed to have reversed themselves. The waves lashed at one another from opposite directions and noisily tossed the wreckage of shattered walls, posts, beams and barrels. The town of Galveston was like a fort after its defenses had been broken through, leaving it exposed to imminent assault. As we viewed the plight of our friends, we were powerless to take a step to help them, for the currents were so strong that it was impossible to brave them.

With the light of day the wind appeared to be diminishing, the storm not quite so violent, we thought—a vain illusion! Of all the buildings located at Galveston, only six had withstood the onslaught of the waves. We saw the breakers against the walls of the hospital where we kept our sick; then the water entered the building. We could no longer stand idle: we dashed into the flood, staying on the highest elevation of ground, managed to reach the hospital, and with untold difficulties conducted the patients to the house of Monsieur Laffitte, which was the best constructed of all on the island.[4] If we had delayed, the sea would soon have taken them off and become their tomb.

The waters still rose. Ships and boats could not resist the constantly re-

---

[4] "The name of Laffitte, the French pirate, has remained notorious; his exploits are often told both in the North and in the South of America. His noble conduct during the invasion of Louisiana by the English in 1815 is well known. The headquarters of this enigmatic person were on Galveston Island. One of his former associates has shown me a tree under which were dug the crypts to contain his buried treasures. After the battle of New Orleans, in which the ruffian was purified of his past existence by a baptism of heroic and patriotic action, he disappeared from view, and it was impossible to ascertain his whereabouts" (GN).

The rank and file of Champ d'Asile never doubted the sincerity of Laffitte's hospitality. Even while giving every outward sign of warm friendship and while supplying material aid, Laffitte was, however, busy informing the Spanish of the colonists' every move and plotting their destruction; the purification achieved at New Orleans did not produce the generous and saintly ally of the French at Galveston whom Gaillardet pictures. His double dealing is convincingly demonstrated by Harris Gaylord Warren, *The Sword Was Their Passport: A History of American Filibustering in the Mexican Revolution,* pp. 202–209, 214, 226, 229.

peated shocks of the waves. They dragged their anchors and soon were carried off to the open sea. A cry of pain and despair which all of us uttered simultaneously began the worst phase of our anguish. We still had stocks of food on several of those vessels; how could we ever recover them? . . . Each of us felt death drawing nearer. Several went to the places of highest elevation, others climbed upon the strongest of the huts to escape drowning. . . . We spent two days in this cruel predicament; the third brought us some relief. The wind let up, the sea returned to its bed, the sky brightened, and toward evening we could reassemble, although there was still a great deal of water which had not yet receded and which formed lakes in various places.

We were truly a touching sight to see. Whenever one of our hapless companions returned to our midst, he was embraced by each in turn and was asked to tell of the dangers he had encountered and of the hopes and fears he had experienced therewith.

Although they survived the flood, the colonists were still beset with troubles. The shortages that previously had loomed ominously over them gradually became more acute and alarming. A part of their already scanty provisions had been lost in the flood, and as an added misfortune their cisterns were now all full of salt water. They could hope to find drinking water only on the mainland, but a bay separated them from it. All their boats without exception had been carried away by the hurricane. One of the colonists fortunately had happened to fill a few barrels with fresh water, by some miraculous forethought, before the cistern had been inundated with sea water. These precious drops of water were divided equally among them all. Two days later a few men went out to explore the island in search of any salvageable debris which might have been cast up after the storm. They came upon two of their boats, which had been abandoned by the waves at some six leagues inland. This was a valuable discovery. From then on they could travel from the island to the mainland and bring a supply of water to last until the cisterns on the island should again become full of drinking water.

As for food, hunting and fishing were the only ways to supply it;

the Indian settlements from which they might have obtained something were between thirty and forty leagues away.

Meanwhile, the pitifully hard-pressed colony received not a word from General Lallemand. It was decided to dispatch the son of General Rigau in search of him. Thirty-two days then passed without any news of either one.

The colony was overcome with discouragement and decided upon a general exodus, with New Orleans named as a future meeting place. Some set out on foot and lived only upon game during a trek of 150 leagues, toward the end of which they received a minimum of help from the sparsely settled population. The elderly, the women and children, and a few officers got passage aboard a schooner that the pirate Laffitte's unfailing generosity placed at the disposal of these wretched castaways.

Thus ended the short history of Champ d'Asile. Thus ignominiously died, fraught with ignominious obstacles, a noble and worthy cause, whose realization might have offered to the world a spectacle of highest interest and achievement. Texas, the Imperial colony, the refuge of many glorious old soldiers, would have occupied in future histories a place alongside the rock of Saint Helena. Its name would have been nobly linked with that great name. For on the one would have lain the remains of the Emperor, on the other, the remains of the Empire, but living, productive remains rising from their ashes to cast seeds of future glory on a land of liberty.

I traveled over a large part of Texas seeking with infinite pains to determine whether any vestige remained of the short-lived settlement of Champ d'Asile. For this purpose I questioned the inhabitants of both town and country, but I could find no one who knew the site of the forgotten field where our Frenchmen made their home for a day. There is such ignorance prevalent among the new population concerning the colony that it is as though a century had passed instead of the short space of time that separates us from it. The few people who seemed to have a faint idea of it recommended that I explore the region around Matagorda Bay, near which is a small settlement with the Spanish name of Refugio. Spanish-settled countries are full of such *refugios,* which bear no connection whatever with the Champ d'Asile of the French colonizers.

Led only by the book of Hartmann and Millard, I went inland along the banks of the Trinity River as far as the town of Liberty. A French-speaking settler in this pleasant new city proved to be, at last, someone to offer help and guidance in my exploration. This good man is a native of Canada who left home to go to New York state. Later he left that state to go to Ohio. After Ohio, he settled in Saint Louis, Missouri, where he developed a thriving fur-trading business with the Indians. As the Indians of that region were no longer savage enough to suit him, he went down to Arkansas, crossed the Red River, and set up his tent right in the midst of the pure-blooded Indians of North Texas. There he lived with his wife and small child for ten years. His home became quite a focal point for the Indians, who either defended or attacked it according to their particular interests at the time. Our Canadian stuck it out and carried on with his unfriendly friends a business punctuated with alerts and rifle fire. "Throughout those ten years," he told me, "I was constantly on my guard, ready for an attack; I kept both by day and by night two horses saddled and bridled in my stable."

In 1832 he bid adieu to the Indians of Texas as he had done to those of Missouri. He went down to the banks of the Trinity, where the colonization had progressed with rapid strides. Today, desirous of ending his days as he began them, by the sea, the old frontiersman is planning to move to the island of Galveston, the mouth of Texas. This location will probably be his last. Once there, he will have described through North America a semicircle of several thousand leagues from north to west and from west to south, with Galveston and Quebec at the two extremities.

My guide was this wandering American who remained French at heart, a man who, having lived in so many places, is nostalgic for only one, France, the one he has never seen except in his mind's eye. Not far from this very town of Liberty, I was at last privileged to re-discover the location of Champ d'Asile. Of the buildings erected by the military colony, there remains not a trace, and I was on the point of turning back with some disappointment when my Canadian friend conducted me opposite some old trees that he pointed to with his finger. I viewed them for a time from top to bottom without noticing anything in particular to warrant our attention. Then my guide showed me some hieroglyphic incisions carved into the trunks and bark of these trees. I went closer, and after studying and deciphering these letters, deformed by sap and by the passage of time, I was able with the help of my guide to make out the words, not with ease but at least with reasonable certainty:

HONNEUR ET PATRIE

This motto is all that remains today of Champ d'Asile, Texas.

CHAPTER ELEVEN

The Story of Pierre Soulé

AT THE TIME of my arrival in New Orleans in 1837, Soulé was regarded as one of the leading lawyers of the city, especially in cases brought before the Court of Assizes. He was married to a lovely Creole girl who belonged to one of the most aristocratic families of Louisiana. His rise to fame and fortune had been rapid. He had recently been named president of a bank,[1] a position which was not considered to be incompatible with his functions as a lawyer, the latter profession not being subject in America to the control which is wielded by the order of barristers and its president.

His house was unrivaled for its hospitality to French visitors of whatever background, whether they came of a well-known family or had acquired some reputation in their own right. I myself received the most cordial of welcomes. My sojourn there coincided with that of Prince Achille Murat, who had emigrated to the United States like so many other members of the Bonaparte family and had determined, like his host before him, to gain admission to the Louisiana bar.

Pierre Soulé, his mentor in his preparation for the bar, his sponsor in New Orleans society, his host who lodged him and his wife, was

[1] This was the Banque des Améliorations.

also generous in providing funds, for the young couple were extremely short of money.

The Prince was not without talent for the bar, but he lacked self-restraint and stability. He was forced to give up his life in New Orleans and withdraw to some city in Florida; not long after, he died. Soulé again displayed his generosity, offering assistance to his widow until she could return to her own family. Pierre Soulé was as great a human being as he was an orator.

He never allowed his friends, and more especially his French friends, to pass through New York without recommending them to me, along with the most lavish compliments. To cite an example:

New Orleans, April 3, 1845

My dear Monsieur Gaillardet:

Permit me to present to your most gracious hospitality two of our compatriots who are traveling northward through the United States and expect to spend some time in New York . . . I would not let them leave me without giving them a note to you. I am eager for them to enjoy an intimacy with the man who for ten years has done the most for the glory of the French name in America and who is himself the most illustrious representative of it.

Since they already admire you, give them the opportunity to love you.
I send them charged with my warmest cordial greetings to you.

PIERRE SOULÉ

When at the close of a session of Congress he wrote me of his own forthcoming visit to New York, I determined to show him that there was really only one illustrious representative, one single glory of the French name in the United States, and that it was not I. I gave a dinner at the restaurant of the Delmonico brothers, the Vefours of New York,[2] to which I invited the elite of the French colony. There I related in a brief speech his accomplishments and his life, already so dramatic and destined to be still more so toward its end. He responded to my toast in tones vibrant with patriotic feeling and then was sur-

---

[2] The Grand Vefour, a leading Parisian restaurant of the nineteenth century, is still in existence today.

rounded and acclaimed with wild enthusiasm. My settling of accounts was complete!

Yet the welcome with which he was received by the French in New York was as nothing compared to that paid him in New Orleans following this first senatorial session, during which he had defended with extraordinary success the principles of the Democratic Party in debate with the celebrated orators, Webster and Clay, who spoke for the Whigs and the Natives.

A banquet was offered in his honor by public subscription, and a toast was proposed by the distinguished organizer of the event "to the man who has just proven that a naturalized citizen can serve and honor this nation fully as well as a native-born citizen."

I shall continue the relation of his career by taking up next our European meeting, his presentation to Prince Louis-Napoleon in Paris, and his duel with the Marquis de Turgot in Madrid.

The senator from Louisiana appeared unexpectedly at my lodgings in Paris in 1850. He had not seen France in twenty years[3] and had seized the opportunity to come there en route to Madrid. He was considering the acceptance of a diplomatic mission to Madrid that he had been offered and wished to make a preliminary investigation there. I shall discuss later the purpose of this mission.

Soulé was naturally eager to become acquainted with the political leaders of Republican France,[4] and especially to see personally the President, against whom he harbored a most distrustful prejudice. I argued with him that his fears were exaggerated. He asked me to introduce him, for he knew that I, like practically everybody, had an

---

[3] "In 1839, Soulé took his family to France where he purchased the Château de Courmes in his beloved Ariège . . . In August [1842] he . . . departed for a holiday in France, where he remained until November" (Amos Aschbach Ettinger, *The Mission to Spain of Pierre Soulé, 1853–1855: A Study in the Cuban Diplomacy of the United States,* p. 108). Gaillardet was unaware of these trips.

[4] The ousting of Louis-Philippe from the throne in 1848 ushered in the short-lived Second Republic, soon to be replaced by the Second Empire (1852).

entrée at the Élysée on Thursday evenings. I told him that it could easily be arranged because of his high office. As a matter of form, I took the precaution of notifying Monsieur Mocquart, the Prince's private secretary, of the liberty I intended to take, supplying credentials of the traveler whom I wished to introduce. However, when I conducted Soulé before the President, it soon seemed obvious to me that Mocquart had forgotten to inform the Prince. What happened was that, when I spoke the words "Pierre Soulé, the United States Senator," Louis-Napoleon bowed very graciously and said to him, "Are you an American, monsieur?" This question was, quite understandably, a blow to Soulé, who had supposed with some justification that his name and French birth would not be completely unfamiliar to one who himself had spent a year in the United States and was a relative of Achille Murat.[5] I quickly broke in, telling the President that Soulé was an illustrious Frenchman in America, a member of the Senate in Washington from a state of French origin. Louis-Napoleon was by nature friendly and polite; he sensed that he had made a blunder, and, therefore, to try to extricate himself from the embarrassment, he asked Soulé the following incongruous question: "Since you are from New Orleans, tell me, what was done about the break in the levee on the Mississippi?"

"It was stopped, monsieur," answered the Senator, with meaningful emphasis on the last two words. The conversation was at an end.

[5] Gaillardet here implies that he mentioned in his note to Mocquart the friendship and financial assistance granted by Soulé to the Murat family. If so, this note may have been enough to account for Louis-Napoleon's strangely cold and somewhat insulting reception of Soulé, regardless of the latter's liberalism. Murat for years had pressed his claim for properties in France of which his family had been dispossessed. In particular, his father Joachim was the original owner of the Élysée palace, the official residence of the French president at which the incident here related took place. If Mocquart or Louis-Napoleon suspected that Soulé represented Catherine Willis Murat, Achille's widow, in a bid for a financial settlement, the Prince's unfortunate reception of Soulé assumes an aspect that Gaillardet could not have suspected. Cf. A. J. Hanna, *A Prince in Their Midst: The Adventurous Life of Achille Murat on the American Frontier,* p. 220.

Soulé immediately grabbed me by the arm, saying, "Let's leave." When we got outside, he raised his arms to the sky and exclaimed, "Poor France, into what hands thou hast fallen!"

The memory of this evening was perhaps not without influence upon another, more serious incident that occurred some years later in Madrid between Pierre Soulé and the Marquis de Turgot.[6] The *coup d'état* of December 2, 1851, had taken place in the meantime. Louis-Napoleon had taken the title of Emperor and had married Mademoiselle [Eugénie] de Montijo, the beautiful Spanish countess. Pierre Soulé had been appointed United States ambassador to Spain by President Pierce. He did not stop in Paris, as he had an aversion to the Empire and the Emperor and was convinced that "that man in the Élysée" felt the same way toward him. Rumor had it that the mission of Pierre Soulé was to bring about the purchase from Spain by the United States of the island of Cuba.

It appears well substantiated that Buchanan, as secretary of state under Polk, did propose to Spain to buy its colony for the sum of $100,000,000. This deal was always opposed by Soulé. He was too firm a believer in the right of peoples freely to dispose of themselves for him ever to approve of their being forced to pay money for this right.

In the speech which he delivered to the Senate on the subject, he made two equally precise and honorable statements. The first was that he "opposed American support of any plot intended to rob Spain of Cuba in violation of the strictest principles of the rights of nations." The second was that he opposed any plan for the purchase of the island and that the idea should be abandoned. He considered it wrong, both for practical considerations and in theory: wrong practically because it would wound both the national pride of the Spanish, a people not willing to be bought off, and that of the Cubans, a people not willing to be sold; wrong in theory because the purchase would be contrary to

[6] Louis-Félix-Étienne, Marquis de Turgot (1796–1866), was successively French minister of foreign affairs (1851–1852), senator (1852), and ambassador to Spain (1853).

the fundamental principles of the American Union, which was established by its founders as a voluntary association of independent states. Soulé was thus of the opinion that the Cuban colony should be allowed to separate from the mother country of its own accord, in the course of time as circumstances dictated, like a ripe fruit dropping off the tree. After that, it would be received into the American Union if it so desired. "But," he added, "the independence of the island would be just as desirable for us as its annexation to our federation. I am one of those who conceal nothing; for truth is not merely a virtue, it is wisdom itself!"

Surely a man who expresses himself so clearly and fearlessly is worthy of our belief.

He was, however, accused of advocating a filibuster policy.[7] Referring to one such accusation by the English Parliament, he made a countercharge against England, as he spoke on the floor of the Senate in Washington. He said that England would do well to look at its own history before throwing stones at others. As an example, he cited a plan preserved in the British archives, under date of May 14, 1739, in which a course of action was outlined to capture the island of Cuba from Spain by the use of forces recruited in the American colonies "at very little cost to England." That this plan was acceptable to the cabinet of Saint James is attested by a letter of Sir William Putney, dated August 27, 1740, in which, referring to Cuba, he says to Admiral Vernon: "Take and keep, let that be our motto. When we shall have captured the island, no one in the world will be in a position to take it away from us." "If then," Soulé added, "we really have the propensity to robber tactics for which the English Parliament blames us, we know from whom we have inherited the trait." The remark was greeted with an outburst of laughter throughout the Senate.

Soulé had, then, no other motive than that of seeking to hasten the day of the emancipation of Cuba through an arrangement between the

---

[7] The anecdote contained in this paragraph is taken from *L'Aristocratie en Amérique*, pp. 247–248. The rest of the present chapter is a translation of pp. 207–210 and 315–324 of the same work.

Cubans and the Spanish. It was a forlorn hope, as Soulé very soon realized. Faced with the uncompromising opposition of Secretary Calderón de la Barca,[8] he could do nothing except forcefully to demand the correction of certain maritime abuses concerning which the United States considered that it had cause for complaint.

Added to the mission to which Soulé was assigned in Spain, he had received another duty from President Pierce and General Marcy,[9] his secretary of state: to study, in conjunction with various other American diplomats in Europe, the political and social climate of the continent and the advisability at that time of granting the support that the European revolutionaries, with [Lajos] Kossuth as their spokesman, were requesting of the American Republic.

This was to be an investigation that the Cabinet in Washington wanted made, without any fixed intention to act upon it but simply as information of no immediate practical value. At Ostend, therefore, was held a conference, or rather a consultation, of the representatives of the United States to the various courts of Europe. Certain of these, notably those assigned to London and Paris, cautiously stayed away, pleading illness. Many absurd reports circulated concerning these secret deliberations, among them the story that Soulé had expressed the wish that Yankee ingenuity would invent a steam-driven guillotine capable of beheading all royalty in one blow. This sort of pleasantry deserves no serious refutation. The fact is that this little conclave, held in the center of the Old World by the apostles of American democracy, resulted in nothing tangible and immediate; instead it paved the way

---

[8] Angel Calderón de la Barca (d. 1861) was appointed Spanish minister to Mexico in 1838. After ten years in Washington (1843–1853), he returned to Spain to become minister of foreign affairs on September 11, 1853. The purpose of the latter appointment was, his wife tells us, to cope with Soulé's diplomacy with regard to Cuba.

[9] Gaillardet correctly refers to Marcy with the title of "General." His biographer states: "In February, 1821, having passed through a series of military grades, he was appointed Adjutant-General of the state [of New York], and thereafter was frequently addressed as 'General' Marcy" (H. Barrett Learned, "William Learned Marcy," in Samuel Flagg Bemis, ed. *The American Secretaries of State and Their Diplomacy,* VI, 153).

for a doctrine, or more precisely a new ambition, whereby the republicans of the United States would no longer abstain from all participation in European politics.

Replacing Washington's rather self-centered isolationism, intervention became a new tendency in American diplomacy, based upon the principle that evangelism is a duty in political as well as religious beliefs. Hence the support given by the United States to various European uprisings, in particular that of the Cretans; hence also its negotiations for the purchase of a port in the eastern end of the Mediterranean Sea, in which undertaking it received the encouragement of Russia, for Russia has long sought in the American Navy an ally against the maritime strength of England and France. Thus is explained why the Polish insurgents were the only ones to receive no help from the United States: an alliance between two governments so different in origin that it demonstrates anew the rule that opposites eventually meet.

Soulé, who was the guiding spirit of the Ostend Conference, had just returned to Madrid when he, along with all the members of the diplomatic corps, received an invitation to a ball given by the French ambassador, the Marquis de Turgot, in observance of some national holiday or other. He attended with his wife and his son, who served as his chief secretary. Mrs. Soulé, as she walked, escorted by her son, past a group of gentlemen, overheard the Duke of Alba say to his friends, "There goes Marguerite de Bourgogne!" I cannot say whether the remark was really said with reference to Mrs. Soulé, but if so, it could have been applied only to her physical appearance. Although she was as beautiful and as buxom as Mademoiselle Georges in *La Tour de Nesle*,[10] she was an honorable woman whose reputation had never

[10] Mademoiselle Georges, stage name of Marguerite-Joséphine Weimer (1787–1867), was one of the most celebrated actresses of her day, from her début at the Comédie-Française (1802) until well into the second half of the century. In 1828 she became associated, both professionally and amorously, with F.-A. Harel (1790–1846), a producer, director, and writer for the Parisian stage. Their liaison continued when he became director of the Théâtre de la Porte-Saint-Martin in 1831. There she played the leading rôle, that of Marguerite de

been stained by the slightest slur of gossip. She, however, read the worst possible interpretation into the words, and her son, going straightway up to the Duke of Alba, challenged him for the insult directed to his mother. The two agreed to a duel.

Upon hearing what had happened, Soulé for his part asked the Marquis de Turgot for satisfaction; he argued that the host was responsible for an insult to a guest under his roof, spoken by the brother-in-law of his chief of state.[11] In vain, the Marquis assured Soulé of his innocence; nothing could dissuade Soulé from the conviction that the scene had been staged against him by or for the Tuileries government, that the insult to him had been intended to please the Emperor and Empress, both of whom had looked upon him as an enemy since the unfortunate outcome of his introduction at the Élysée. How strange are the effects of preconceived notions!

The first duel took place without injury either to the Duke of Alba or to Soulé's son; in the second, a bullet lodged in the Marquis de Turgot's knee, from which he remained lame for the rest of his life.

This regrettable encounter rendered difficult the continued presence of Pierre Soulé at the Court of Madrid.[12] Moreover, he failed to receive from General Marcy the full support he had been promised. He therefore requested his recall, and in order to show to the satisfaction of young America that his conduct had been consistently firm and loyal, he published his diplomatic correspondence with the Cabinet in Washington. This did him honor, but his mission had failed, and in politics success is the only important thing.

Bourgogne, in Gaillardet and Dumas's *La Tour de Nesle.* See Arthur Pougin, "Georges, Mlle," *La Grande Encyclopédie.*

[11] Emperor Napoleon III and the Duke of Alba were married to sisters, the daughters of the Countess of Montijo (cf. Calderón de la Barca, *Attaché in Madrid,* p. 18).

[12] The chronology was actually as follows: the Turgot ball, November, 1853; the Black Warrior affair (here referred to as "certain maritime abuses"), spring, 1854; the Ostend Conference, autumn, 1854; Soulé's resignation as minister, December, 1854. As we suggest in our introduction, it is the sympathetic interpretation of Soulé's character and motivation that is of value here, not the exact, factual information. For the latter, Gaillardet exhibits a sovereign disregard or else a very hazy memory—a disciple of Dumas to the end.

His replacement in the Senate had been necessitated by his mission; he therefore had lost his seat. He withdrew to relative obscurity until the outbreak of the Civil War. In line with the policy he adhered to, he disclaimed the epithet of "disunionist" with which the late Henry Clay branded him, and strove with all the strength at his command to keep Louisiana within the framework of the Union. His popularity suffered accordingly. However, although he felt compelled to hold out so long as only two or three states had announced their secession, he became convinced that he could not withstand the general current when nine states formed a new confederacy. Revolt was then transformed into revolution.

When the fortunes of this gigantic but unequal struggle of four million men on one side against thirty million on the other brought the Northern fleet and armies before New Orleans, and a capitulation became inevitable, Soulé received from the authorities the task of negotiating the surrender. This painful mission he accepted and performed with equal dignity and patriotism. The bitterness which consumed him burst forth, however, in the proclamation that he was assigned to write to the people of New Orleans to recommend their submission to fortune's decrees. In it, the losing side stood up one last time and hurled into the faces of the victors the most violent reproaches for the pitiless harshness of their terms.

General Butler was the principal target of this last attack of a dying cause. He could not forgive Soulé for it, and in return did his utmost to humiliate him, trying to force him to take some sort of oath, which however Soulé refused to take. Then General Butler had him placed under arrest and conducted to Fort Lafayette, in the harbor of New York. President Lincoln was more equitable, gave the ex-senator credit for the spirit of moderation that had characterized his actions in the insurrectional movement in Louisiana, and released him from prison on condition that he would leave American soil until further notice.

Soulé took refuge in Havana. As he was a person unable to remain long idle, he conceived a plan for obtaining for himself and a company of capitalists and shipbuilders the franchise for the operation of all the customhouses of the ports of Mexico, then a new empire. This was the reason for his several voyages to Mexico. His purpose was not, as has been erroneously stated, to resettle there a large group of Southern planters.[13] The latter project was the work of a Mr. Gwin. Neither of these plans could be brought into effect, owing to poor Emperor Maximilian's hesitancy to act.

Soulé was finally granted permission to return to New Orleans. The bar there again echoed his mighty roars; the lion had grown old but still was strong and majestic. A series of private griefs succeeding his political misfortunes with overpowering speed did at length crush altogether this magnificent creation of nature.

He unexpectedly lost his wife, who was still young and whom he loved as the finest and most devoted of spouses. Shortly after that, his only son, the husband of a lovely Creole from one of the first families of Louisiana and the father of two small children, was struck with madness. Beneath the weight of personal tragedy coupled with patriotic anguish, the old statesman himself felt his reason give way; this great intelligence was undermined; this man of outstanding energy, courage, and ability went mad. He had been in a state of physical and moral prostration for over a year, when death mercifully intervened in 1870. God granted him the grace of sparing him the knowledge of the disaster in France. His son followed him to the grave in 1878.

This life, which so early was exposed to the turmoil of politics, which began in exile, which reached the pinnacle of fortune in the greatest of all republics, and which ended in neglect and madness, teaches us most dramatically both the power and frailty of the human mind. It strikingly demonstrates too the futility of partisan struggle, in which so many questing souls, so many brilliant thinkers in the Old as well as the New World, without gain either to themselves or to their country, are needlessly sacrificed.

[13] "In 1865 he joined ex-Senator William M. Gwin, of California, in a project to settle Confederate veterans in Sonora, Mexico" (Ettinger, *Mission to Spain,* p. 473).

APPENDIX

Concerning Pierre Soulé in Madrid
Passages Extracted from Fanny Calderón de la Barca's
The Attaché in Madrid, or Sketches of the Court of Isabella II

The author of Life in Mexico during a Residence of Two Years in That Country, *Señora Calderón (1804–1882) published also her diary of life in Madrid in 1853–1854. She was present at the Turgots' ball when Madame Soulé was insulted, and recorded the event. We reprint here from her work* The Attaché in Madrid *the pages which are concerned with Soulé. Her version and Gaillardet's concur in the main, but disagree as to the motive for the duels; Gaillardet was in a better position to know what was going on in Soulé's mind. As the insult to Madame Soulé was in the form of a comparison of the American minister's wife to Gaillardet's own dramatic heroine, Marguerite de Bourgogne, the episode remained particularly vivid in his mind when, twenty-five years later, he wrote his account. It is entirely possible also that he had access to Señora Calderón's book and wished to correct her inaccuracies (e.g., the misnomer "Marie de Bourgogne") and to present what he thought to be a truer account.*

Of Scottish origin, Señora Calderón wrote this diary in English, but published it anonymously, slightly altered, representing it as a translation from the work of an unnamed German diplomat. In later life she became the governess of the Infanta Isabella, the eldest child of the Queen of Spain, Isabella II. (See Henry Baerlein, introduction to Señora Calderón de la Barca's Life in Mexico.*)*

October [1853]

The great topic of conversation at present in Madrid, is the arrival of the new American minister, Mr. Soulé, a red-hot democrat, whose late speeches in his own country, in favor of the annexation of Cuba, have naturally excited a vast amount of prejudice against him, in this. It seems to us a strange nomination on the part of the President of the United States. Perhaps in a democratic government there was only the *embarras du choix*, as it may be inferred that other public men there have the same sentiments, though less openly and offensively expressed. He is said to be a man of talent, a Frenchman by birth, a *républicain rouge*, who was obliged, on account of his political principles, to leave his native country, where he was known as the editor of a republican newspaper, entitled "The Yellow Dwarf," *le nain jaune*. He will require much tact and prudence to overcome the prejudice universally felt against him. His secretary of legation, Mr. Perry, is married to a very charming poetess, *La Coronata*. Count A——— is of the opinion that the nomination of Calderón de la Barca to the post of minister of state was partly intended as a kind of counterbalance to that of Mr. Soulé, it being supposed that his long residence in America will enable him to see through the political intrigues with which it is supposed that the latter functionary intends to distinguish his diplomatic career.

He called this morning at the legation, when I happened to be present. He has a very remarkable countenance; dark, deep-set eyes; his hair cut after the fashion of the ancient French republicans. He is very polished in his manner, and speaks well—slowly, in rounded flowing periods. As the French say, *il s'écoute en parlant*. He seems very desirous to make himself agreeable, but is, perhaps, somewhat too confident of his own powers. (pp. 72–73)

*   *   *

I have been so much engrossed in these matters, that I have forgotten to give you an account of the great ball given at the French Embassy on the day of Ste. Eugénie, in honor of the empress, a few days before the opening of the Cortes. The Countess de Montijo, who had prepared her beautiful salons to celebrate the same event, waived her right to the representatives of France. On that evening, at least, diamonds were taken from their cases and saw the light, and it would have been difficult to find a greater combination of beauty and magnificence in any ball-room. Of course, all that was most distinguished in Madrid composed the assembly, and as the rooms were crowded, I was amused to hear the complaints of the old Condesa de ———, that many had been omitted who should have been invited. "Better for them and for us," said I. "By no means," said the old lady. "Better that we should all stifle, than that any one should be offended." Between the intervals of a quadrille and a waltz, I observed the American minister, Mr. Soulé, standing alone, and apparently in rather an isolated position, and it struck me, that though the most polite attention was shown to him and his family by the host and hostess, there was not much anxiety manifested to make his acquaintance. "He has only himself to thank," said M———. "If you were informed that a man had been urging his neighbors to rob your house, you would not feel very cordially disposed towards him. But the Spaniards are a good-natured people, and I have no doubt they will soon forget their motives of complaint against him, if he is prudent and conciliating. There are some very good-looking people here to-night," continued M———, who as usual had taken up his post of observation in a corner, with his back against the wall. "That little Countess S———o———i is a nice little independent-looking thing, a good rider, a good shot, and yet no *lionne*; besides caring no more how she looks than I do." "Fortunately she is extremely handsome, and some one dresses her remarkably well. Then she dances like a zephyr." "But after all," said M———, "one does not see that high-bred air amongst the women, which we find in a London party of the same standing." "They are *so* much prettier here," said I, "so much more graceful, so much more *piquantes*. When did you ever see such feet in London?" "Possibly never, but there are very few such *grandes dames* here as we have in London." "I disagree with you. There are none who have so much pretension, and they are not *fenced off* as these ladies are in London. But they are quite as *grandes dames*, and perhaps in reality quite as proud of their old names and families, as your London duchesses."

"I am not to be convinced. There is not the air of high-breeding that the English women have, not that look of *race* which we see amongst the daughters of our aristocracy. In fact there is no very marked difference here between the wives of the bankers and merchants, and the señoras of the *sangre azul*." "I think M——— is right in the latter remark," said C———s, "but I draw a different inference from this circumstance. I think it proceeds from the fact, that those of a secondary class here are always ladylike, and in England this is not invariably the case; especially when they happen to meet with the higher class in society, and look as if they felt themselves out of place. On these occasions, your great ladies are apt to look high and condescend-

ing, and the others fluttered and embarrassed, from an exceeding desire to
appear quite at their ease." "Two against one," said M——; "nevertheless,
I hold to my opinion."

A few minutes afterwards, I happened to form one of a group of *pollos*,
amongst whom was the Duke of Alva. They were very merry, and making
remarks, critical or laudatory, upon all the world as they passed,—upon the
beauty, the toilettes, &c., especially of the girls and young married women.
Amongst others who passed us, was the lady of the American minister,
dressed, I think, in dark green velvet, and leaning on her son's arm. "Here,"
said the duke in French, "comes Marie [sic] de Bourgogne." Some one
whispered to him that the lady was French, and he turned away and changed
the conversation.

Alas! what mighty ills from little causes flow! As it turned out, the young
man had heard the remark, and treasured it up as a matter of grave offence.
Want of knowledge of the world—for he seems very young—and the idea
of an intentional offence to his mother, may plead his excuse. Be that as it
may, it seems that he left the assembly, boiling with rage, and determined to
make it a matter of life and death between himself and the duke. Fortunately, some cooler head than his own prevented him from making an
esclandre in the ball-room. It seemed a night famous for indiscreet remarks;
for a little while after, as the handsome young Duke of F——a was leading
his partner to a chair, she exclaimed—"I want you to look at the most
ridiculous dress! Observe that lady with rubies and diamonds, and such a
baroque-looking gown, of every color under the rainbow." "So it is," said
the young duke; "I told my mother it was frightful, but she insisted upon
wearing it." The young lady was shocked; but her partner, laughing heart-
ily, went up to his mother. "Mamma," said he, "everybody thinks your
gown a fright." "I am sorry for everybody's taste," said the marquesa, good-
humoredly, "for I think it a beauty."

Notwithstanding these *lapsus linguae*, the ball continued with great ani-
mation, and was kept up till four in the morning. As for the brilliancy of
the toilettes, it would require a fairer hand than mine to do them justice.
"We particularly remarked," as the English newspapers say, the magnificent
dress of the Countess of Montijo, although, except her being in one blaze of
diamonds, and wearing on one arm a bracelet of large gray pearls—a gift, I
was told, of the emperor—I cannot pretend to give any description of her

costume. The *corps diplomatique* and cabinet ministers were, of course, in full uniform. All the remarkable generals and statesmen were present, and if politics were discussed in corners, which no doubt they were, there was at least no outward demonstration of any thing but careless enjoyment. Busts and pictures of the heroine of the fête were dispersed through the rooms. "*That* is an aristocratic head, you will allow," said I to M——, as he was leaving the supper-room. "Because she has Anglo-Saxon, or at least Scotch blood in her veins," replied he triumphantly.

Even the debates, even the ministers, even politics seemed forgotten, swallowed up in the excitement caused by two duels, following each other, and all proceeding from a velvet gown! It appears that the supposed intentional insult of the Duke of Alva to Madame S——, rankled in the mind of her son, and both father and son agreed that an apology must be demanded. All remembrance of the remark had, no doubt, passed away from the duke's mind, and he was preparing to set out with a party, consisting of various members of his family, to church, to assist at the baptism of his baby, of which, I believe, her majesty was to be the godmother, when he received a note from young Soulé, which, after hastily reading, he immediately answered, disclaiming all intention of giving offence to Madame S——é, all recollection even of having remarked upon her toilette, and a total ignorance of having even seen her; regretting, however, that he should inconsiderately have said any thing which could give the slightest offence to a lady. It was supposed, therefore, that the matter was satisfactorily adjusted; but somehow or another, it was whispered about, and repeated by good-natured friends, that the young man was crowing over his having forced an apology from the Duke of Alva, and that imputations were thrown out against the courage of the latter; and so, from less to more, the matter grew serious, and a challenge was sent by the duke and accepted.

Every one had gone that day to the *rifa* or raffle, an affair got up upon a great scale for the benefit of the poor, under the direction of a society composed of the principal ladies of Madrid. It was held in La Trinidad, formerly a convent, now belonging to the department of *Fomento*; and for months preparations had been making for it. One could not enter a house where the young ladies were not embroidering, or pasting, or drawing, or manufacturing something for the *rifa*. It was somewhat in the style of the fancy fairs which I have seen in London, only every thing was drawn by lot.

Of course the blanks bore a most disproportionate majority to the prizes; but as it was for the poor, to provide them with coals and clothing during the winter, no one was allowed to complain.

The first ladies in Madrid presided at the various tables. The Duchess of Gor, Countess of Montijo, Marquesa de Malpica, and others, were the presidents, and distinguished by a lilac ribbon tied round their arm. It was their office to receive the tickets that had been drawn, and to have them compared with a book in the charge of a clerk, where the corresponding numbers were marked. If it was a prize, they directed the lucky individual to the table where the article was marked with the same number. I admired the indefatigable patience of these ladies, who sat in this great hall day after day, from morning till night, unrolling tickets, answering questions, and attending with unwearied politeness to every individual who came up to them.

All classes were there, from the highest to the lowest. One table was especially dedicated to beautiful gifts, sent by the Queen, the King, the Ynfante Duchess of Montpensier, and the little Princess of Asturias. Of course every one was desirous to gain something from this table; the watch and chain of the queen, the opal bracelet of the Ynfante, and so on. I had taken tickets for at least a dozen young ladies, and neither they nor I had won any thing excepting a remarkably ugly yellow pincushion, which I insisted upon transferring to E—— C—— V——, one of the handsomest girls in Madrid, when C——s came up, and whispered to me that a duel was to take place that day between young Soulé and the Duke of Alva, and that they had gone out to the country; the duke's seconds being Gen. Concha and the Count of Piñon-Rostro, and those of his antagonist, Mr. Perry, Secretary of Legation, and the fiery Milaus del Bosch.

I looked towards the Duchess of Alva, who, with her exquisitely beautiful little boy beside her, was unconcernedly unrolling a number of tickets which she had taken; and at the Countess of Montijo, who was opening papers for a young countryman with a pretty girl by his side; and felt certain that the report had not reached them.

We went to the Casino in the evening to hear the result. Neither were wounded. They fought with swords, which were found too heavy, and exchanged for lighter ones. Of course there were a thousand versions of the particulars, but the important fact was, that the duel, a foolish quarrel for a foolish cause, was well over.

Although some very important political events have occurred, I shall give you an account of them afterwards, and so fill up a gap in my journal. But now I must leave you to imagine the astonishment of the Madrid world, when it was announced, that not satisfied with the reparation to his wounded honor which had already been given, Mr. Soulé had challenged the French ambassador! This was a more serious business than the first. That two young men should have a *rencontre*, did not excite much surprise, absurd as it was, the cause considered; but that two men of advanced age, the one a minister plenipotentiary, the other ambassador and *doyen* of the diplomatic corps, should upon the same subject, was rather out of the usual way. The letter from Mr. Soulé, which appeared in the *Illustrated London News* some days afterwards, I copy for your edification.

Monsieur le Marquis:—

The difference which has arisen between the Duke of Alva and my son, took place in your *salons*. It was at your house, where I and my family were invited guests, and on the occasion of a fête of which the Duke of Alva might consider himself in some measure the hero, that the latter insulted Madame Soulé, without any thing having hitherto happened to exonerate us from the bond of good fellowship, which that circumstance causes to weigh upon you [sic; *read* "which causes that circumstance to weigh upon you"]. It is even positively asserted that the insulting expression afterwards made use of by the Duke of Alva, and so nobly taken up by my son, first proceeded from your mouth. That being the case, Monsieur le Marquis, I have a right to go to the true source which placed swords in the hands of the Duke of Alva and of my son, to make it mine as far as you are concerned, and to demand personally a satisfaction which you cannot refuse me. Mr. Perry, an American citizen, and my friend, is charged to receive your reply. I have the honor to be, Monsieur le Marquis,

Your very humble servant,
PIERRE SOULÉ,
Citizen of the United States

December 17th, 1853.

As might be expected, the answer from the marquis, *un vieux militaire,* was not conciliatory. A challenge was returned by the emissary, and Lord H——n agreed to act as second. The duel was fixed for a certain day. The project got wind. The government was resolved to do all in their power to prevent its taking place. Lord H——n being informed of this, considered it a point of honor to hasten the affair, and the combatants accordingly stole a march upon the authorities. The result was that a ball was lodged in the ambassador's knee, and as it has not yet been extracted, considerable uneasiness is felt by his friends as to the result. The Soulés have flown at high game; but that this will advance their social position, or render Mr. Soulé's diplomatic duties more easy, remains to be proved.

In almost all cases of this nature, sympathy is felt for the sufferer, but more especially where, as in this latter instance, his opponent is the aggressor. This is actually the one topic of conversation in Madrid, and various are the motives attributed to Mr. Soulé for having sought this meeting. The whole of Madrid, without exaggeration, have made inquiries at the Embassy, the diplomatic corps of course amongst the first. The reception-room of the Marquise was crowded this morning. She seems very courageous, and thankful that it is no worse, though likely to be very lingering; and it is probable that, in the way of entertainments, their hospitable house is shut for the season. I was told by M——, who had it from an American gentleman, that Mr. Soulé, who was as cool as if going out to breakfast, remarked just before the duel began, "I shall not kill M. Turgot; I shall merely put a ball in his knee." (pp. 119–127)

BIBLIOGRAPHY

Almanach administratif, historique et statistique de l'Yonne, année 1883.
Auxerre: Albert Gallot, 1883 (biographical sketch with portrait of Gaillardet, Part II, pp. 46–48).

Calderón de la Barca, Frances Erskine. *The Attaché in Madrid, or Sketches of the Court of Isabella II.* New York: D. Appleton and Co., 1856.

———. *Life in Mexico during a Residence of Two Years in That Country,* ed. with intro. by Henry Baerlein. New York: E. P. Dutton and Co., Inc., 1931.

Chambers, Henry E. *A History of Louisiana: Wilderness, Colony, Province, Territory, State, People.* Chicago and New York: The American Historical Society, Inc., 1925.

Chase, Mary Katherine. *Négociations de la République du Texas en Europe, 1837–1845.* Paris: H. Champion, 1932.

Chevalier, Michel. *Lettres sur l'Amérique du Nord: Extraits,* ed. Robert G. Mahieu. Princeton, New Jersey: Princeton University Press for Institut Français de Washington, 1944.

Chinard, Gilbert. "Les Expériences américaines de Victor Jacquemont," in *Jacquemont.* Paris: Museum d'Histoire Naturelle, 1959.

Connor, Seymour V. and Virginia H. Taylor, eds. *Texas Treasury Papers: Letters Received in the Treasury Department of the Republic of Texas, 1836–1845.* Austin: Texas State Library, 1955–1956.

Dresel, Gustav. *Houston Journal: Adventures in North America and Texas, 1837–1841,* tr., ed. Max Freund. Austin: University of Texas Press, 1954.

Ettinger, Amos Aschbach. *The Mission to Spain of Pierre Soulé, 1853–1855: A Study in the Cuban Diplomacy of the United States.* New Haven, Conn.: Yale University Press, 1932.

Fortier, Alcée. *A History of Louisiana.* New York: Manzi, Joyant & Co., 1904.

Fournel, Henri. *Coup d'œil historique et statistique sur le Texas.* Paris: Delloye, 1841.

Fromageot, J. "Un Tonnerrois 'éruptif' de l'époque romantique," *L'Écho d'Auxerre,* No. 56 (mars–avril, 1965), 23–30.

Gaillardet, Frédéric. *L'Aristocratie en Amérique.* Paris: E. Dentu, 1883.

————. "Des Attributions du Président des États-Unis," J.-P.-O. Commettant, *Trois Ans aux États-Unis: Études des mœurs et coutumes américaines.* II. Bruxelles et Paris: Pagnerre, 1857.

————. *Georges, ou le Criminel par amour,* drame en 3 actes par feu Lebras et M. Frédéric Gaillardet. Paris: Barba, 1833.

————. *Mémoires du chevalier d'Éon, publiés pour la première fois sur les papiers fournis par sa famille et d'après les matériaux authentiques déposés aux archives des affaires étrangères.* Paris: Ladvocat, 1836.

————. *Mémoires parus sur la chevalière d'Éon: la vérité sur les mystères de sa vie, d'après des documents authentiques.* Paris: E. Dentu, 1866.

————. *Profession de foi et considérations sur le système républicain des États-Unis, présentées aux électeurs de l'Yonne.* (campaign pamphlet, 1848)

————. *Réplique imprimée à une réponse manuscrite de M. Pernelle.* (pamphlet on local politics at Le Plessis-Bouchard, 1869) Paris: Renou et Maurde, n.d.

————. *Struensée, ou Le Médecin de la reine,* drame en cinq actes. Paris: Barba, 1833.

————. *La Tour de Nesle,* drame en cinq actes et en neuf tableaux, par MM. Gaillardet et x x x [Alexandre Dumas]. Paris: J.-N. Barba, 1832.

Gaillardet, H. Introductory biographical notice on Frédéric Gaillardet by one of his descendants in *Mémoires du chevalier d'Éon.* Paris: Grasset, 1935.

Gayarré, Charles. *Essai historique sur la Louisiane.* Nouvelle-Orléans: B. Levy, 1830–1831.

————. *History of Louisiana: The French Domination.* New York: William H. Widdleton, 1866.

————. "The Louisiana Bench and Bar in 1823," *Harper's Monthly Magazine,* LXXVII (November, 1888), 889–900.

Hackett, Charles Wilson, ed. *Pichardo's Treatise on the Limits of Louisiana and Texas.* Austin: University of Texas Press, 1946.

Hanna, A. J. *A Prince in Their Midst: The Adventurous Life of Achille Murat on the American Frontier.* Norman: University of Oklahoma Press, 1946.

Hartmann and Millard. *Le Texas, ou Notice historique sur le Champ d'Asile, comprenant tout ce qui s'est passé depuis la formation jusqu'à la dissolution de cette colonie, les causes qui l' ont amenée et la liste de tous les colons français avec des renseignements utiles à leurs familles.* Paris: Béguin, 1819.

Hubert-Robert, Régine. *L'Histoire merveilleuse de la Louisiane française: Chronique des XVIIe et XVIIIe siècles et de la cession aux États-Unis.* New York: Éditions de la Maison Française, Inc., 1941.

Jefferson, Thomas. *The Papers of Thomas Jefferson,* ed. Julian P. Boyd. Princeton, New Jersey: Princeton University Press, 1950——.

——. *The Writings of Thomas Jefferson,* ed. Andrew A. Lipscomb. Washington, D.C.: Thomas Jefferson Memorial Association of the United States, 1904.

John, George O'Brien. *Texas History: An Outline.* New York: Henry Holt and Co., 1935.

Kellogg, Louise Phelps. "Jolliet, Louis," *Dictionary of American Biography.* New York: Charles Scribner's Sons, 1933.

Kennedy, William. *Texas: The Rise, Progress, and Prospects of the Republic of Texas.* London: R. Hastings, 1841.

Lamar, Mirabeau B. *The Papers of Mirabeau Buonaparte Lamar,* Volume V, ed. Harriet Smither. Austin, Texas: A. C. Baldwin & Sons, 1921.

Larcher, Albert. "A Propos du célèbre et énigmatique Chevalier d'Éon," *L'Écho d'Auxerre,* No. 50 (mars–avril, 1964), 27–30.

Lauvrière, Émile. *Histoire de la Louisiane française, 1673–1939.* Baton Rouge: Louisiana State University Press, 1940.

Learned, H. Barrett, "William Learned Marcy," in Samuel Flagg Bemis, ed.

The American Secretaries of State and Their Diplomacy, VI, 143–294. New York: Pageant Book Co., 1958.

Leclerc, Frédéric. *Texas and Its Revolution,* ed., tr. James L. Shepherd, III. Houston, Texas: Anson Jones Press, 1950.

Little, Katherine Day. *François de Fénelon: Study of a Personality.* New York: Harper and Bros., 1951.

Maissin, Eugène. *The French in Mexico and Texas (1838–1839),* ed., tr. James L. Shepherd, III. Salado, Texas: Anson Jones Press, 1961.

Martin, François Xavier. *The History of Louisiana, from the Earliest Period, with a Memoir of the Author by Judge W. W. Howe, to Which Is Appended Annals of Louisiana, from the Close of Martin's History to the Commencement of the Civil War, 1861, by John F. Condon.* New Orleans: J. A. Gresham, 1882.

Monaghan, Frank G. *French Travellers in the United States, 1765–1932.* New York: The New York Public Library, 1933.

Moraud, Marcel. "Le Champ d'Asile au Texas," *The Rice Institute Pamphlet,* XXXIX (April, 1952), 18–44.

―――. "The Diplomatic Relations of the Republic of Texas," *The Rice Institute Pamphlet,* XLIII (October, 1956), 29–54.

Newcomb, W. W., Jr. *The Indians of Texas: From Prehistoric to Modern Times.* Austin: University of Texas Press, 1961.

Newell, Chester. *History of the Revolution in Texas, Particularly of the War of 1835 & '36, Together with the Latest Geographical, Topographical, and Statistical Accounts of the Country from the Most Authentic Sources.* Austin, Texas: The Steck Co., 1935.

Pougin, Arthur. "Georges, Mlle," in *La Grande Encyclopédie.* Paris: Librairie Larousse, n. d.

Prévost, M. "Bertin l'Aîné," *Dictionnaire de biographie française,* VI. Paris: Librairie Letouzey et Ané, 1954.

Rémond, René. *Les États-Unis devant l'opinion française, 1815–1852.* Paris: A. Colin, 1962.

Rowland, Dunbar. *History of Mississippi: The Heart of the South*. Chicago-Jackson: S. J. Clarke Publishing Co., 1925.

Soulié, Maurice. *Autour de l'aigle enchaîné: Le Complot du Champ d'Asile*. Paris: Marpon & Cⁱᵉ, n. d. [1929].

Stiff, Edward. *The Texan Emigrant: Being a Narrative of the Adventures of the Author in Texas and a Description of the Soil, Climate, Productions, Minerals, Together with the Principal Incidents of Fifteen Years Revolution in Mexico and Embracing a Condensed Statement of Interesting Events in Texas, from the First European Settlement in 1692, down to the Year 1840*. Cincinnati: G. Conclin, 1840.

Texas in 1837: An Anonymous, Contemporary Narrative, ed. Andrew Forest Muir. Austin: University of Texas Press, 1958.

Tinker, Edward L. "Mazureau, Etienne," in *Dictionary of American Biography*. New York: Charles Scribner's Sons, 1933.

Tourneux, Maurice. "Gaillardet, Frédéric," in *La Grande Encyclopédie*. Paris: Librairie Larousse, n. d.

Walker, Henry P., ed. "William McLane's Narrative of the Magee-Gutiérrez Expedition, 1812–1813," *Southwestern Historical Quarterly*, LXVI (October, 1962), 234–251; (January, 1963), 457–479; (April, 1963), 569–588.

Warren, Harris Gaylord. *The Sword Was Their Passport: A History of American Filibustering in the Mexican Revolution*. Baton Rouge: Louisiana State University Press, 1943.

Webb, Walter Prescott, ed. *The Handbook of Texas*. Austin: The Texas State Historical Association, 1952.

Williams, Amelia W. "A Critical Study of the Siege of the Alamo," *Southwestern Historical Quarterly*, XXXVI (April, 1933), 251–287; XXXVII (1933–1934), 1–44, 79–115, 157–184, 237–312.

Wortham, Louis J. *A History of Texas from Wilderness to Commonwealth*. Fort Worth, Texas: Wortham-Molyneaux Company, 1924.

Yoakum, Henderson K. *A History of Texas from Its First Settlement in 1685 to Its Annexation to the United States in 1846*. Austin, Texas: The Steck Co., 1935 (facsimile of original dated 1855).

976.4 NewOr History
976.335   History

976.335 Customs

INDEX